The Country of Language

THE *CREDO* SERIES

A *credo* is a statement of belief, an assertion of deep conviction. The *Credo* series offers contemporary American writers whose work emphasizes the natural world and the human community the opportunity to discuss their essential goals, concerns, and practices. Each volume presents an individual writer's *credo*, his or her investigation of what it means to write about human experience and society in the context of the more-than-human world, as well as a biographical profile and complete bibliography of the author's published work. The *Credo* series offers some of our best writers an opportunity to speak to the fluid and subtle issues of rapidly changing technology, social structure, and environmental conditions.

The Country of Language

Scott Russell Sanders

Scott Slovic, *Credo* Series Editor

Credo

MILKWEED EDITIONS

Published 1999 by Milkweed Editions
Printed in Canada
Cover design by Wink
Cover photograph by Darrell Eager
Author photo by Eva Sanders Allen
Interior photographs provided by Scott Russell Sanders
The text of this book is set in Stone Serif.
99 00 01 02 03   5 4 3 2 1
First Edition

Milkweed Editions, a nonprofit publisher, gratefully acknowledges support from our World As Home funders: Lila Wallace-Reader's Digest Fund; Creation and Presentation Programs of the National Endowment for the Arts; and Reader's Legacy underwriter, Elly Sturgis. Other support has been provided by the Elmer L. and Eleanor J. Andersen Foundation; James Ford Bell Foundation; Bush Foundation; Dayton Hudson Foundation on behalf of Dayton's, Meryvn's California, and Target Stores; Doherty, Rumble and Butler Foundation; Dorsey and Whitney Foundation; General Mills Foundation; Honeywell Foundation; Jerome Foundation; McKnight Foundation; Minnesota State Arts Board through an appropriation by the Minnesota State Legislature; Norwest Foundation on behalf of Norwest Bank Minnesota; Lawrence and Elizabeth Ann O'Shaughnessy Charitable Income Trust in honor of Lawrence M. O'Shaughnessy; Oswald Family Foundation; Ritz Foundation on behalf of Mr. and Mrs. E. J. Phelps Jr.; John and Beverly Rollwagen Fund of the Minneapolis Foundation; St. Paul Companies, Inc.; Star Tribune Foundation; U.S. Bancorp Piper Jaffray Foundation on behalf of U.S. Bancorp Piper Jaffray; and generous individuals.

Library of Congress Cataloging-in-Publication Data
Sanders, Scott R. (Scott Russell), 1945–
    The country of language / Scott Russell Sanders. — 1st ed.
       p.   cm.
    Includes bibliographical references.
    ISBN 1-57131-229-3 (cloth). — ISBN 1-57131-230-7 (paper)
    1. Sanders, Scott R. (Scott Russell), 1945– . 2. Sanders, Scott R. (Scott Russell), 1945– —Knowledge—Language and languages. 3. Authors, American—20th century—Biography. 4. Language and culture—United States. I. Title. II. Series: Credo (Minneapolis, Minn.)
PS3569.A5137Z465 1999
818'.5409—dc21
[b]   99-18336
                                           CIP

This book is printed on acid-free, recycled paper.

For my teachers, living and dead.
—SRS

The Country of Language

The Country of Language

The Country of Language

by Scott Russell Sanders

The Gift

I was visiting an elementary school near Cincinnati one day, reading to well over a hundred children in the gymnasium and telling them stories about the history of the Ohio Valley. I wore a creamy linen shirt with a wide collar and blousy sleeves, black peg-legged trousers, battered leather boots, and a weary felt hat, the whole outfit meant to suggest the garb of a backwoods peddler from early in the nineteenth century.

Most grown-ups would have rolled their eyes at my costume and my ham acting, as I told of steamboat races and run-ins with bears and blizzards and river pirates, but the kids, more tolerant, just perked up their ears. They were sitting on a hardwood floor, so I could judge the effect of my little show by how much they squirmed. They squirmed a fair amount, but every once in a while, as I turned a surprising corner in some tale, they grew absolutely still. In those moments, the children and I slipped away from the scuffed gymnasium, away from the ticking of clocks, into the world of story, where we glimpsed in a clear

3

light some remarkable person, some worthy gesture, some wild creature.

At the end of the program, while I was gathering my books and props, a redheaded boy of eight or nine sidled up to me and said, "Mr. Sanders, I know you like thinking about the old-timey days."

"I sure do," I told him.

"So I brought you this." The boy stretched out his palm to offer me an arrowhead, a wedge of pewter-gray flint veined with red, gleaming and sharp as though freshly made.

"It's a beauty," I told him, taking the stone point and running my fingers gingerly along the scalloped edges. "Where'd you find it?"

"On my grandpa's farm. I look there every spring after the plowing."

"Well, you found a dandy one," I said. "In fact, it's so perfect I think you'd better hang onto it."

I tried handing the arrowhead back to the boy, but he thrust his fists into the pockets of his jeans and shook his head.

A tall woman in a blue print dress who had been lingering beside the stage, and whom I had taken to be a teacher, now stepped forward. "He's got a whole drawer full of them at home," she said, "and he picked out this one especially for you. He'd really like you to have it."

"Then I'll put it with my treasures," I told the boy, closing my hand around the cool, sharp stone.

"My grandpa died," the boy said abruptly. He studied me to see what I would make of this fact.

I gazed back at his freckled face and hazel eyes, unsure how to make the loss any less bewildering. "Did he help you hunt for arrowheads?"

The boy dipped his chin but said nothing, his lips pressed tight. I asked if he would let me give him something. He looked up at his mother, who nodded yes, and then he nodded. So I pulled out a copy of my book about the frontier peddler, a man who appears in the illustrations dressed roughly the way I was that day, with slightly more of a paunch and a good deal more beard. I asked the boy his name, and he told me, and I wrote it in the book: "For Charles, who remembers his grandpa."

I keep the arrowhead now on the shelf beside my writing desk, alongside pebbles and shells and seeds and water-smoothed chunks of wood, each one a memento of some place that left its mark on me, some lesson learned. The lessons I live by have come to me piecemeal, unexpectedly, like the gift of that arrowhead. They don't add up to a philosophy; they don't form a tidy system of ideas that could be diagrammed on a chalkboard or numbered on a list. They're more like a grab bag of stories, each one capturing a moment of insight when some heart's truth came home to me. I can't fully separate the insights from the experiences that gave rise to them. In fact, I'm wary of abstract theories and creeds that hover in thin air. My beliefs are rooted in ordinary, earthy life. What follows is a sampling of the stories that guide me, told as briefly and directly as I can tell them.

Bitten by the Wild

On our farm outside of Memphis when I was three, newly arrived in the country of language, I climbed into a backyard apple tree one hot day and met a long, skinny, slithering creature for which I had no name. It was like a living length of rope. I poked it with my bare toe, to see what it would do, and one knobby end of the rope snapped at my leg. A sharp pain made me wail.

Mother came rushing out of the kitchen, found me in the tree, and swept me into her arms. What is it? she demanded. What happened? I couldn't say, could only clutch my leg and writhe. She peeled my fingers away, saw the puncture marks in the skin of my calf. Then she carried me swiftly back into the house, into the bathroom that smelled of lotions and soap. Balancing me on one hip, she bent down and opened a faucet in the tub. The sound of water pouring and the trembling in my mother's arms hushed me. She called my sister, who soon came running. Sandra would have been seven that summer, a big girl in my eyes, and I longed to do everything that she could do. Mother told her to fetch some ice from the refrigerator.

By the time the ice arrived, Mother had pulled off my shorts and plunked me into the tub. The water was cold, and I flinched, trying to scramble out, but she held me down. My leg throbbed. As she was dumping tray after tray of ice into the tub, Sandra peppered her with questions, but Mother only said to go get Daddy. My hurt leg had turned as red as apples and it looked twice as big around as the good leg and the skin felt tight. There wasn't enough air in the room. My head whirled.

Presently my father came in, sweaty from chores, followed by Sandra, panting, and by the two hunting dogs, who were never allowed in the house. Then I heard my mother say *snake,* a word new for me, and at last I had a name for what had gone wrong. *A snake bit him,* Mother said. She pointed at the aching leg, and when I looked at it I didn't see how the swollen thing could belong to me. It was a log covered in red bark, a slab of meat from the freezer, a stuffed pillow, but not my leg. A weight on my chest made breathing hard. I looked up from the chilly water to find blue and red lights dancing on the walls. And then the room faded and my breath quit and I left the world.

Nearly fifty years later, Mother recalls things differently, Dad's not around to ask, and Sandra remembers nothing of that day at all. How could you forget? I say to my sister. Your little brother was in agony. You brought ice. You may have saved my life. Sandra only smiles indulgently and says she'll take my word for it. Mother agrees that I did nearly die from shock after the snakebite, but claims she would never have dunked me in a tub of ice water. She would have sucked venom from the wound and packed my leg in ice and bundled me in blankets to keep me warm and taken me straight to the hospital. But I recall no blanket, no hospital. I remember lying there shivering while the dogs dangled their wet pink tongues over the edge of the tub and Dad went out to grab a hoe from the barn to kill the snake. No, Mother insists, Dad was building tires at the Firestone plant, and the dogs would have been outside where they belonged, and the snake bit me next to the woodpile, not in any tree.

Which is only to say that memory is a trickster, shifting shapes, playing jokes, reworking the past. It may be that I moved my serpent from the woodpile into an apple tree after hearing in church about the Garden of Eden. Or I may have sent my father out with the hoe because, in later years, I saw him chop off the heads of other snakes. I must have painted in the color green, because it doesn't match the color of any poisonous snake from Tennessee. Whatever actually happened on that day in the summer of 1948, the version I've told here is the one that comes back to me when I close my eyes.

It wasn't the last time in childhood that I nearly died, but it may have been the closest call. The wonder is that falling unconscious from snakebite and suffering for days from a swollen leg didn't make me wary of playing outdoors, didn't make me fearful of animals, didn't even spook me about snakes. Mother claims that I was the stubbornest boy to bring indoors, and I believe her. There were so many things out there to see and sniff and touch, so many butterflies to chase, birds to watch, pebbles to collect, grass blades to chew on, hills to roll down. Meals would get cold while everybody hollered for me and I took my own sweet time in coming inside, even though I knew the price of my dawdling might be a spanking.

A few months after meeting the snake, not long after my fourth birthday, I tagged along behind my father and one of his hunting buddies when they trooped off across our land with their bird dogs in search of pheasants. Father told me to scoot back in the house, and I did, until the two of them and their dogs passed over the ridge of the cow pasture, and then I went tearing after them. Father spied me trailing him again and he turned back a few steps, warning that he would jerk a knot in my tail, and so I turned back, too, but only far enough to hide. When they went on, I went on. At the edge of the pasture they crossed through a barbed-wire fence, which was as far as I had ever wandered before, and I crossed through after them into a brushy field. I kept on following them until their long legs outstretched mine, and for a spell I followed their voices, and then I could only hear the banging of shotguns—a sudden, jumpy sound that might have come from anywhere— and then I couldn't even hear the guns. I ran on a ways, then slowed to a walk, then stood still.

"I've never been lost," my father used to say, "but there's been a few times when I didn't know where anybody else was." Standing in that shaggy field, where the bushes rose higher than my head, I sure didn't know where anybody else was. Up to that point in my life I had never been out of sight or sound of at least one person who loved me. Instead of being terrified, as I should have been, I was amazed. The world kept going on, every step of it different from any step I had taken before, and there were places like this field chock full of things to look at but empty of people. I sat down in a grassy patch and began searching for bugs.

Before I ran out of bugs to examine I heard Mother's voice yelling my name. Then I heard Sandra's voice, high-pitched and worried. Only when my father began shouting did I realize I was in trouble. I didn't think to yell back. Staying lost seemed less risky than being found. But soon there was a crashing in the tall grass and the bird dogs came galumphing up to me, their whole bodies wagging with delight. They kept looking back over their haunches, expecting someone, and sure enough, in a minute here came my father, long thin feathers jutting from the pocket of his hunting coat, the shotgun broken open at the breach and tilted over his shoulder. From studying his face as he bent down to me I couldn't tell whether he was happy or mad. No matter how closely I stare at that blurred memory, I still can't tell.

When I think back over the scenes that have shaped me, the most vivid ones take place in woods and fields and along stony creeks, in sunshine or rain or snow or in the speckled shade of trees. Even today, when I earn my living almost entirely indoors, I feel a steady hankering to be outside. It's as though the snake that bit me left some of its wildness in my veins.

For as far back as I can remember, I've never

doubted that I'm an animal, just one more curious, hungry creature alongside all the others. I've always understood that my flesh is made from other flesh. On our farm we ate chickens that had scratched in the yard and pheasants that once lay on the kitchen counter wrapped in their shining feathers like a coat of stars. We ate potatoes we had dug from the ground like soft brown stones. We drank milk from a cow whose flanks felt warm against our cheeks in the winter barn. Because we buried rabbits and turtles and goats, I've known from an early age that I will die. Unlike my father, I admit to having been well and truly lost, in cities and suburbs as well as wilderness. Instead of panicking, I try to welcome those moments, give up chasing after distant voices, forget my destination, be still, and discover where I am.

Words

In one of my earliest memories I'm toddling beside a railroad track and singing "Chattanooga Choo-Choo" for all I'm worth, hoping that if I sing hard enough a train will come chugging along. Presently a train does come along, rolling backward, first the caboose and then dozens of boxcars and then the huge black engine with its plunging pistons and grinding wheels. A man with a drooping moustache leans from a window in the locomotive and waves his blue cloth cap at me, as if to acknowledge that I alone, by the power of my singing, have dragged him backward down the tracks.

And why shouldn't my voice be able to summon up a train? By calling *Mama* I could almost always bring my mother, and *Daddy* would sometimes bring my father, and my sister's name or the names of our dogs would often bring them running. I could lean against the board fence of our neighbors' paddock and call the name of their old draft horse, and he would come ambling up to lick salt from the palm of my hand with a raspy tongue. I could say *snake* and see in my mind the green rope coiled in the crotch of a tree. I could say *plum* and taste the fruit in my mouth. I could say *creek* and smell the mud. Every last thing in the world had a name, I realized, a string to hold it by. I spent my days gathering up those strings.

The stories my father told about his boyhood days on the back roads of Mississippi were filled with words that he kept in his head and that I soon carried in mine: *mule, moonshine, rapscallion, snuff.* Even more words lived in books. Mother turned the pages and found there long stories which I would ask her to say over and over again, and each time I listened closely to make sure the words didn't change. Before long, Sandra was bringing picture books home from school to practice her reading on me. As she ran her finger across the page, I tried to find words hidden in the squiggly black marks. If I grew hungry for a story when Sandra was away at school and my father and mother were busy, then all I could do was leaf through books on my own, murmuring the words as I remembered them.

In another early memory, I look out from the barn doorway to see a cloud of green tickets fluttering down from an airplane. I rush out to snatch one and discover that the paper slip is covered with those inky marks—a wonderful gift from the sky, if only I could read. I turn it over and find on the other side drawings of a chair and a couch and a rocket ship. The couch and chair leave me cold, but the rocket inspires me to wonder if the tickets might be announcing an invasion of earth from outer space. No sooner do I imagine the possibility than I decide it must be so. Why else would an airplane drop scraps of paper on the whole countryside? With a wind of fear swirling in my belly, I gather up a handful of tickets and go running to the house, where I find Mother outside the back door pulling weeds from a flower bed. I show her one of the tickets and before I can draw breath to tell her what I fear, she reads calmly:

"Calhoun Furniture Showroom Grand Opening."

"Is that all it says?" I ask her.

"It gives prices for things and directions to find the store and the hours when they're open."

"What about the rocket ship?"

Mother turns the ticket over and studies the picture. "That? It's just a come-on, sweetheart. To make you think how up-to-the-minute they must be."

If I wanted to avoid being tricked by pictures, if I wanted to feed myself stories whenever I grew hungry, I would have to learn to read. I begged Sandra to teach me how, and I kept on begging, with the persistence of a hungry chick, until she agreed. So every afternoon I waited beside the road with our collie for the school bus to arrive, and when Sandra climbed down, the dog and I followed her to the screened porch of our farmhouse, where she opened a book and gave me reading lessons.

Naturally, we began with the alphabet. When I discovered that there were twenty-six letters, I thought I would never live long enough to memorize so many, and I asked Sandra if I could get by with eight or ten. No, she said, I needed all twenty-six, even *q* and *z,* and she patiently taught me the whole alphabet. I drew their shapes on paper, in the dirt, in the palm of my hand. Then she showed me how those letters hooked together to form words, how words hooked together to form sentences. And so at the age of four, safe on that porch while mosquitoes and wasps and flies ticked against the screen, I began to read. *The snake bites my leg. The train rolls down the track.* Suddenly those ink marks on paper set whole worlds moving inside me.

Learning to write came a good deal more slowly than learning to read. I understood how to make letters easily enough, but to make them one after another wore me out. My fingers cramped; my arm seized up. My mind raced on ahead faster than I could push the pencil. So when I began spinning stories of my own, Sandra offered to write them down. On the screened porch after supper we would make up long tales featuring Bear and Frog and a boy and girl named Mason and Dixie. Their adventures usually began at our back door, but the four companions might wind up in California or Africa, on the North Pole or the Moon. They got into scrapes, took turns saving one another, and saw the most wondrous things. Some days, everything else that happened to me seemed pale beside the bright light of those stories.

All the while our dog Rusty took almost as many hours of reading and writing lessons as I did. He lay beside us listening or nuzzled our laps as Sandra and I studied, his tongue dripping on the page. Yet he never learned even the first letter. I tried briefer experiments with the cow, the billy goat, a pet raccoon, and a rabbit, with the same results. This did not fool me into supposing that animals are dumb, for I had seen all of them do amazing things; it merely convinced me that reading and writing must be our own best tricks. We couldn't run as fast or jump as high, couldn't hole up all winter underground, couldn't make honey from flowers or dams out of sticks, couldn't fly like birds or swim like fish, couldn't do a thousand fabulous things the other animals could do; but we could read, we could write, we could name everything under the sun.

Pony

When I was five my family moved to the Ravenna Arsenal, an Army munitions plant in the northeastern corner of Ohio. Within the arsenal's chain-link fence, herds of deer browsed on grassy bunkers filled with bombs, hawks circled over an airfield where fighter jets landed, beavers built dams in creeks rainbowed with slicks of oil, and foxes dug burrows near the dump where old shells exploded at dusk. Pictures of the animals came into my head when I heard in Sunday school about Adam and Eve naming the beasts in their garden, or when I heard about Noah loading all of the creatures, two by two, onto his ark.

I loved the animals but feared the bombs. Who knew when a bunker might blow? Who knew when a man packing explosives into shells on one of the load lines might stumble and blast the whole building to smithereens? I feared the swiveling radar screens that swept the air with their blank eyes. I feared the guards who stood by the arsenal gate with pistols on their belts or cruised the perimeter of the fence in shark-tailed Chevrolets. I feared the Army tanks whose treads gouged the dirt. Unlike the trains that stuck to the rails as they rumbled past our farm in Memphis, these big machines could go anywhere, and they paid no attention to me. If I got in their way, they would squash me like any beetle or mouse.

Fear did not keep me from roaming to the far corners of the arsenal over the next few years, but it sharpened my senses. I kept a lookout for guards prowling in their olive-drab cars. I watched for signs bearing a skull and crossbones. I noticed fish floating belly-up in lakes, noticed bare patches of ground where nothing grew, noticed every bloodied clump of feathers and glistening bone. As I was learning in school to read books, in the arsenal I learned to read the woods and fields.

In one of those far fields, beyond the load-lines that rattled night and day churning out shells for the war in Korea, a wrecked bomber lay moldering. Grapevines and blackberry shoots laced through the fuselage and stalks of bright orange butterfly weed rose up through gaps in the wings. With friends I often climbed into the cockpit to play at killing. Once I was there alone, staring through a cracked windshield, my hands on the control levers, when a plump-bellied pony the color of cinnamon came stealing toward the nose of the plane. There was an alertness about him that I had never seen in the horses back on our Tennessee farm. He would snatch a clump of grass in his yellow teeth, jerk his head up and swing it around to scan the field, then he would take a few cautious steps forward, sniff the air, and bend down for another bite of grass. Cockleburs knotted his tail and mane, and a shaggy forelock draped down over his eyes. Hidden by the crazed glass of the windshield, I sat tight and watched him come.

He was beautiful and spooky and wild—but he was also a handy enemy. So I picked up from the floor of the cockpit a chunk of steel, the housing for some shattered gauge. The pony must have sensed the movement, for he lifted his head, flared his nostrils, and stared up at the plane. The whites of his eyes showed through the tumble of cinnamon hair. A tremor rippled the pelt over his ribs. Afraid he would bolt before I could launch my bomb, I thrust my arm through a hole in the roof and heaved the lump of steel at him. As the missile flew, the pony laid back his ears and bared his teeth, and when it landed, far short, he wheeled violently and galloped away.

For an instant I felt as brave as any hero in the movies, driving the enemy before me. And then I felt ashamed. I never told my father or mother, never told the friends who played war with me, never told anyone until now.

For some years after hurling that make-believe bomb at the pony I would keep on playing war, but in the future I would use for enemies only monsters I had imagined—storm troopers whose visors hid their faces, dragons from the depths of earth, aliens from outer space. And then eventually, after I had moved from the arsenal, I would grow sick of slaughtering even imaginary enemies, and I would begin to study peace. I would become a conscientious objector during the Vietnam War, a decision that bewildered my father and mother, and I would protest against that war, against the government that waged it, against the culture of killing that I knew from my days in the paradise of bombs.

On the day I tried to kill the pony, as soon as the

hoofbeats died away I climbed down from the cockpit and searched for the jagged chunk of steel, as if by retrieving it I could undo my act. But the grass was too long, the briars too thick, and I had to live with what I had done.

Looking

My chief teacher outdoors was my father, who took me for long, ambling walks through the Ohio countryside. He marveled over everything alive, including the dirt, which he often scooped up by handfuls and sifted through his fingers. Sometimes he would rub a pinch of dirt into his palm, feeling the texture, and then he would lick it, comparing the taste with other soils he'd known. He never crossed a patch of mud or a field of snow without scanning for animal tracks. Here was another alphabet for me to learn, with many more than twenty-six letters: the sharp, two-pronged imprints of deer; the four dots for rabbits, with one hind leg trailing the other; the raccoon's track shaped like a baby's plump hand; the dimpled footpads of squirrels; the splayed footpads of fox; the small scrapings of mice.

My father cared less about creatures that did not wear fur, such as frogs and worms and grasshoppers— all of which fascinated me—and the only birds that interested him were the ones he could hunt, such as pheasant and quail and ducks. Above all other wild things he loved trees. They were steady and faithful, he told me. Trees found everything they needed right where they stood, without having to run all over creation like animals. Often on our walks he would take me to see a particular tree that impressed him— a black walnut, maybe, or a shagbark hickory—and he would introduce us, boy and tree, as if we were two people met on a street corner. Without his ever saying so, I realized that my father thought of trees as persons, dignified and deep-rooted, and that was how I came to think of them as well.

Now, when I write about hugging the solemn maples in my backyard, or about stroking the grown-up willows that my father and I planted long ago, or about seeing the creamy branches of a sycamore as voluptuous, readers will occasionally send me letters asking if I really love trees that much. I assure them that I do. Their bewilderment is as puzzling to me as my affection for trees is puzzling to them.

We treat with care what we love, and we love only what we have truly learned to see, with all our senses alert. When he sawed and sanded and hammered in his basement workshop, my father treated wood with the same respect that he gave to the flesh of deer under his skinning knife. I learned from him that we have no choice but to use the bodies of other creatures, so we should use only what we need. We should waste little, clean our plates, save every scrap of wood. We should give thanks for all that we receive, never take a blessing for granted, never suppose that a single living thing deserves to die for our sake. Everything alive wishes to keep on living, my father taught me, so I'd better have good reason before I cut short a life.

As I learned to recognize animal tracks and tree bark and leaf shapes from my father, so I learned the alphabets of flowers and vegetables and fruits from my mother, who was always the gardener. No sooner did we move into the arsenal than she began planting scarlet salvia and purple phlox, lettuce and tomatoes; no sooner did we move out of the arsenal, when I was nine, to a small farm a mile or so beyond the fence, than she started planting all over again. Her blossoms drew hummingbirds and butterflies and bees. Nothing alive was too small to engage her, including the one-celled squirmers that we looked at under the bright light of a brass microscope handed down to us from her physician father. She taught me to delight in pattern, no matter the scale, from the veining of a leaf to the branching of a stream, from the curl of an amoeba's false foot to the sweep of the Milky Way.

Many of the lessons I received from my mother took place indoors, as she was fixing supper or mending clothes or reading a book. Unlike my father, who could remain silent for long stretches of time and who, in his preoccupation with a job, often would not hear what I was saying to him, my mother was always ready to listen and talk. Whereas my father hardly ever spoke about his feelings, my mother spoke frequently about hers, including pain and anger as well as joy, and she encouraged me to speak about mine. Much disgusted her—the stench of a rotting carcass, the racket of rock music, any allusion to sex—and much delighted her—the smell of new-mown hay, the rumble of thunder, any polite reference to God. You never had to guess her reaction to anything under the sun, for she would tell you swiftly and frankly.

Around the time we moved from the arsenal, my

sister Sandra's Girl Scout troop went to camp for a week, and my mother agreed to go along and help, which meant that I had to go along as well. I moped through the first day. At the age of nine I thought of girls as belonging to a separate tribe, one whose language and behavior I could scarcely understand. Even Sandra had become mysterious to me. All that first day at camp my mother tried to interest me in what the girls were doing, but I would not braid lariats, would not sketch wildflowers, would not stagger on a rope bridge across a creek. I sulked. I lay on my cot reading *The Last of the Mohicans*. I sat on a stump and whittled a branch into the shape of a musket.

At length night fell, leaving me only six more days of exile to suffer through in this gathering of girls. While they sat around in the main cabin singing jolly songs, I stood at the screen door with my back to them, staring into the darkness. Lightning bugs winked on and off, on and off, like the neon sign at the truck stop where our country road met the highway. Bullfrogs croaked. Locusts fiddled.

From the circle of singers my mother called, "Don't you want to join us, sweetheart?"

I shook my head no and pressed my cheek against the screen. Just then a shape flew at me out of the darkness and I leapt back, heart thumping. A moth, drawn by the lights in the cabin, had landed on the screen. It was pale green, as wide as my hand, with a white furry body and spots like tiny eyes on the undersides of the wings, which tapered into long curving tails.

I had to show this marvel to someone before it flew off, so I ran to fetch my mother. She came away from the singing and bent down to look through the screen.

"Why, it's a luna moth," she said. "I haven't seen one in ages!" She turned around and called for the others to come see, and they left off their singing and trooped over. In a moment I was surrounded by jostling girls. "Look what Scott found," my mother said. "Isn't it magnificent?"

The girls murmured. Most of the boys I knew would have wanted to catch that moth or stick it on a pin or scare it into flight. But the girls were content to look. Their voices rang with wonder, and that sound made them seem less strange.

Hunger for Books

On the main street of Ravenna, the county seat eight or nine miles from our home near the arsenal, there was a brick library with white pillars out front and row upon row of books inside. In the hushed air of that place I could read about luna moths or glaciers, I could find pictures of how girls looked without their clothes, I could study formulas for rocket fuel or maps of where the Indians lived, could follow any question wherever it led, and all for free. We had to pay at the movie theater and bowling alley and miniature golf course, we had to pay at all the stores, we even had to pay at the Methodist church when the offering plate came by, but the library was like the grade school or the woods, free to anybody who cared to walk inside.

I visited the library once a week, first with my mother, and then, when Sandra learned to drive, with my sister, and eventually on my own. Early on, I chose my weekly reading downstairs, where the children's books called to me from the midst of banners, mobiles, stuffed animals, and model dinosaurs. Perhaps because of those models, at first I imagined that all of these books had been made ages ago, like fossils, and that all of the people who wrote them had long since died, and that authors, like dinosaurs, were now extinct.

Then on one of my visits I noticed a shelf labeled "New Books." Curious, I drew out a shiny volume, opened it gingerly, heard the stiff spine creak, ran my fingers over the unblemished pages, lowered my nose to smell the fresh glue and ink. Then I opened another and another. They were indeed brand new. But where had they come from? When I asked the librarian, she explained that authors, unlike dinosaurs, were far from extinct. In fact, she said, thousands of new books were published every year. At that moment, standing in the children's room of the library in Ravenna, Ohio, I realized that if there were still people writing such fresh and fragrant books, then maybe one day I could write some as well.

All these years later, after making more than twenty books of my own, I still feel the miraculous power in language, whether written or spoken, the same power I felt when I sang a train into motion and I learned the name of *snake* and Sandra taught me the alphabet on the screened porch of our farmhouse in Memphis. How extraordinary, that a few sounds or a few squiggles can rouse up people and voices and landscapes in our minds! Like sunshine, like the urgency of spring, like bread, language is so familiar that we easily forget what an amazing gift it is.

Today, using a library that contains millions of volumes, I recognize that my childhood library in Ohio, which seemed so enormous, was actually quite small. It seemed enormous to me because, week by week, year by year, I passed through those library doors into the great world of human thought and art and story. Reading the books I found there, I went on adventures; I dived under the sea and climbed mountains; I met explorers and baseball players and scientists; I learned the names of rocks and birds and butterflies; I learned how to build log cabins, how to launch model rockets, how to trap muskrats; I roved through the past and all over the earth and even beyond the earth; I studied the planets and the stars; I dreamed my way to the beginnings of time and to the ends of the universe.

A library is a storehouse, preserving what humans have learned, generation by generation, in every land, but it is a storehouse with doors and windows and hallways opening outward to the vast, sprawling, worldwide treasure trove of human knowledge. Surely this is what most clearly distinguishes us as a species, the ability to accumulate knowledge and to pass it on. We pass it on by word of mouth, we pass it on by example, we pass it on in films and tapes and disks, in magazines and newspapers, but above all we pass it on in books.

Libraries have become, of course, much more than houses for books. They've become knots in the global web of information. However, in this age of new devices for storing and transmitting knowledge—from videotapes to CD-ROMs, from cable television to the Internet—I'm still devoted to the humble book. A book requires no electricity. It is portable, made for the hand and pocket. It invites but does not demand our attention, and it leaves us time to think. We can enter or leave a book just as we choose, and we can interrupt our reading to burp a baby or pay a bill or ponder a cloud. A good book appeals to what is best in us, without trying to sell us anything. Books may become dated, of course, yet never because of some shift in technology or because their parts wear out, and the best of them are more durable than any manufactured product.

I'm not foolish enough to believe that books will survive merely because I love them, or because I write them, or because they've shaped my life. By comparison with films or videos or computer bulletin boards, a good book requires more from us in the way of intelligence and imagination and memory, and that makes it vulnerable to its glitzy competitors; but a book also rewards us more abundantly. The best books invite us to share in a sustained, complex, subtle effort to make sense of things, to understand some portion of our humanity and our universe. As long as there are people hungry for such understanding, there will be people hungry for books. My own hunger set in long before I could read, back when ink marks on the page were still an impenetrable mystery, and yet even now, after devouring so many thousands of books, I am as ravenous as ever.

Garden

I learned to exult in the power of words not only by naming animals, in the manner of Adam and Eve, and not only by summoning up a loud and noisy train with my small singing voice, but also by reciting lists of baseball players, fighter jets, chemical elements, and cars. I stuck labels on fossils I dug from the creek, on arrowheads I found in the plowed fields, on the flyleafs of books, on jars full of coins. During those early days in the country of language I drew no distinction between things made by people and things made by nature. I simply went out to meet the world, seeking the words to map it all into meaning. I wandered about with questions on my tongue and my ears tuned for answers. In the library or in the woods, at home or in school, I wanted to climb every branch in the tree of knowledge and gobble every fruit I could find.

If I keep thinking about the Garden of Eden as I recount some of the experiences that shaped me, it is most likely because I started writing these pages in a setting filled with the furniture of paradise. While visiting an old mill town in northern Vermont for a week in June, I sat every day at a round table under an apple tree, tapping at lettered keys while ducks and doves and smaller birds pecked for food near my feet. This was not a recollected apple tree, like the one in Tennessee hiding the green snake that bit me, but a present one, on which I could lay my hand between sentences. A strip of lawn bordered by gangly, exuberant flowers—ox-eye daisies, foxglove, daylilies, pink spires of lupine, luminous yellow coreopsis—stretched away on either side of me. Bees nuzzled the blossoms. Every now and again toads hopped from their shadowy niches onto the grass to meditate in splashes of sunlight. Beyond the frowzy border of flowers and saplings and blackberries the land tilted down to the granite trough of a river, which was roaring after days of rain, and just there, close enough for me to feel mist on my face as I wrote, the water tumbled over a ledge to form a churning cauldron of froth.

When I arrived for my week's visit, the purr of falling water was the first sound I heard on opening the door of my guest room in the old mill. I walked straight through to the bedroom and swung open the windows and the soft ruckus swept over me. It was like the sound of sand shaken in a pan, like the brush of a thousand brooms over a wooden floor, like the vast exhalation of a great animal that never sleeps and never runs out of breath. Waking and sleeping, all that week I wrapped myself in this liquid music. How could I keep from thinking of Eden?

Paradise would surely need such a brimming river, such a waterfall, for no sound could speak more directly to the soul. The settlers of this green valley in Vermont may have felt the same, because they named the river Gihon, after one of the streams—there are four of them—that flow from Eden in the Book of Genesis. The name in Hebrew means a gushing forth, as of water rising in a spring.

No heavenly angels plucking harps could have played more beautifully than this river stroking stone. I soaked in the sound. And yet every few minutes I realized that I'd stopped hearing it, and then I would look up, see the roiling foam, open my ears once more, and there it was, the roar of the falls. The river kept offering its gift whether or not I was paying attention. To hear it steadily, without any wavering of pleasure or gratitude, would be perfect mindfulness, full awakening.

My deep delight in the sound of moving water goes back, like most of what I cherish and most of what I fear, to childhood. When I was a baby my father used to carry me onto the porch whenever it rained, and the harder it rained the longer we stayed. As soon as I could rove about on my own two legs, I would run to the porch at the first rumble of thunder, or I would race over the grass to stand in the door of the barn while a storm pounded the roof. I'm still drawn to rain, rapids, waterfalls, or fountains, to any purring of water. The sound goes through me, dissolves the hard little cinder of the self, and leaves only the one vast current surging.

What is that attunement of self and world if not an intimation of paradise? I have felt it often, not only in the presence of moving water or ghostly moths or nervous deer, but also in shimmering trees, in meadows of stars, in grasses swept by wind, in a chorus of crickets; and not only in meetings with nonhuman nature, but also in passages of music and poetry, in the elegant findings of science, in the sharing of food and talk with people I love; I have felt it indoors and out, in company or in solitude.

If what I glimpse in these moments is paradise, the fulfillment of my constant hungering for wholeness, then paradise is all around us all the time, had we but eyes to see. It is as though most of the time we grow numb to the splendors of our dwelling place, as my ears grew accustomed to the exquisite ruckus of the Gihon River, and only occasionally do we come awake to behold what is truly and always here. This is one of my deepest and oldest intuitions, that one current courses through all things. I sensed this permeating presence before I learned any religious language to speak of it, and I sense it still, after I have grown wary of all the names for God.

Grief

Why notice a toad basking in sunlight while babies shiver in dank hovels? Why marvel over a moth while bloodshed fills the headlines? Why celebrate the bounty and beauty of creation while humans suffer from ugliness and want? Those are fair questions. They've led critics to complain that writers who dwell on nature must be indifferent to society, with all its glories and ills, as if nature and society were two rival camps. Even if you dwell on the human sphere, critics may charge you with ignoring their own favorite cause. I've been told that anyone who writes about marriage, as I do, thereby overlooks divorce; that anyone who examines life in towns neglects the needs of cities; that anyone who speaks of devotion to place ignores the ache of uprooting; that anyone who traces the search for a spiritual center must know nothing of our current confusion.

I confess to ignorance on many grounds, but not to ignorance of grief. The grief I know is only in small part my own, because I've been spared the worst thus far, but I've seen every manner of suffering in neighbors' houses, I've seen hatred up close, I've seen bruises and squalor and waste. I've known addicts and alcoholics, suicides, deserters and those they deserted, and the victims of slow, wasting disease. I've also lived through more than half of this violent century, and ever since I learned to read or to follow grown-up talk I've felt in my bones the relentless chronicle of poverty, hunger, racial strife, murder, theft, abuse of women and children, epidemics, war. I would never mistake the world we've made for utopia. I would not pretend that nature is nice. The wilderness I knew as a boy was laced with poison and sown with bombs.

No matter how much I write about the possibility of peace and commitment and love, I bear in mind the threat of cruelty, the certainty of pain and loss. I never forget that we have been kicked out of Eden, that we must labor to fill our bellies and to bring forth our young, and that every living thing must die. So I write always in the face of grief. I write about hope because I wrestle with despair. I describe glimpses of paradise as a measure of what we might aspire to and of the direction we might go. To write about the natural order that sustains us is not to ignore the human condition, but to insist on our most fundamental needs—for light and earth and water and air, for companions, for beauty, meaning, grace.

Early one morning while I wrote under the apple tree beside that waterfall on the Gihon River in Vermont, a great blue heron came gliding upstream and landed on the far bank, just across from where I sat. The bird folded its gunmetal gray wings, stepped gingerly down on its stilt legs to the water's edge, then stood in profile to me, long orange beak jutting out, white face tapering away to a black plume. For a minute or so the heron aimed at me its yellow unblinking eye. Then the long beak swiveled in my direction, and for a minute more the heron fixed me with its hunter's gaze. I did not move. The bird stood still. The river poured over the falls.

It's true that while I locked eyes with the heron I didn't think about the greasy slicks that coiled above the falls nor the dingy suds that gathered below. I didn't think about the men and women without jobs in that depressed mill town, nor the children across our country thrashing from nightmares in their beds, nor the shuffling refugees in distant lands, nor the victims of rape, the starving, the weeping, the mad. For that brief spell I scarcely thought at all.

Then a garbage truck on a nearby street began to groan, crushing a load of trash, and suddenly the heron unfolded its wings, bent those long legs, and leapt into the air. In a few heartbeats it was gone.

I took a breath, and there I was again, sitting at a round table under an apple tree with my fingers on a keyboard and my bare feet in the grass. The world swept back over me, with its reminders of wounding and healing, misery and recovery. My communion with a bird did not make me indifferent to the human lot; it restored my sanity, my courage, my awareness of our fellow travelers who share the earth with us, each kind going its own distinctive way.

On my own way home from Vermont after that week in the old mill, I waited in the Burlington airport, sitting off by myself near a window. Sunlight covered my lap. I opened a book and the pages glowed as if lit from within. As I began to read, I withdrew from the din of loudspeakers and the bustle of travelers and I entered the realm of words, where I've spent much of my life. Though I was gazing at nothing more than ink marks on paper, a voice rose from the page and captured my attention, reasoning and recollecting, telling stories, speculating on the truth of things.

The book didn't seize quite all of my attention, however, for as I read I noticed a shadow flicker across the sunlit page. Glancing up, I saw a butterfly beating its way past the window, flimsy as a leaf, buffeted by turbulent air, angling down as though to land on the runway among the brawny trucks and planes. From the flash of yellow and black I guessed it was a tiger swallowtail. While I watched, a cargo jet came lumbering in for a landing, wheels lowered, descending at the same angle as the butterfly. For an instant both aircraft were framed in the window, the tiny insect and the giant machine, then both cruised away out of sight.

I closed the book and sat there in a wash of sunlight musing on what I had seen. Although the conjunction of butterfly and jet was merely accidental, it set me thinking about the polarities of my life, the tug-of-war in my heart between nature and artifice, between loving the order of things and loving what we do with that order. I revere the grand constellation of powers that made the butterfly, love the creature itself and the fierce, dazzling energy of its flight through this dangerous world; yet I also honor the human skills required to build and fly the plane, to weave an invisible web of radio and radar messages, to carry goods and people through thin air.

If you had asked me when I was ten or twelve or fourteen what I wanted to do when I grew up, I would not have mentioned writing books. Most likely I would have told you that I wanted to build rocket ships and fly them to other planets. During high school I read everything I could find in the library about space travel, I filled notebooks with sleek designs, I dreamed of meeting alien creatures in remote constellations. The universe I hoped to explore began outside the atmosphere of earth.

But the earth kept calling me. When I tried my hand at trapping muskrats as a boy in Ohio, I felt about equal admiration for the cleverness of those who invented the hair-trigger traps and for the cleverness of the muskrats in evading them. When I stalked with my father as he hunted in the arsenal, I marveled over the deadly precision of shotguns, and over the sly speed of rabbit and deer. When I studied elementary physics, I gloried over the way that human formulas could embrace the whole universe, but I also wondered at our own minor planet, which is more intricate than any map. As I grew skillful enough to catch muskrats, I lost my desire for catching them; as I grew old enough to carry a shotgun of my own, I lost my taste for hunting; as I came to recognize the tyranny of equations, I became wary of science the way I had become wary of religion.

There's no philosophical or emotional difficulty in loving both the contrivances of wildness and the contrivances of mind, but there is a practical one. The more cargo jets fill the sky, the fewer the butterflies;

the more garbage trucks, the fewer herons. The more thoroughly we dominate the planet, with our technology and our numbers, the less freedom there is for other creatures to flourish. If we spend enough time in air-conditioned rooms listening to our own voices or watching electrons dance on screens, we might easily suppose that nature is now our captive, our dependent, framed by our purposes, as that butterfly was framed by the airport window. But that would be a dangerous illusion. No matter how many fences we build, no matter how many lines or numbers we draw on maps, no matter how much concrete we pour or chemicals we spray, we are not in charge and never will be. We are the guests of a great and mysterious power. That power, in all of its myriad manifestations, is my abiding subject. In writing about nature, I am not turning my back on society; I am seeking to place our small, brief lives within the vast encompassing order on which our every breath depends.

The Real Questions

As I raced through high school, chasing ideas and basketballs and girls, everybody who knew me felt certain that I would study mathematics and science in college, most likely physics, because I was obsessed with uncovering the secrets of the universe. The school principal, the guidance counselor, my teachers, the minister at church, the commander at the arsenal, my parents and my friends, all agreed that I was destined to become a scientist. How could I think otherwise?

My sure future was complicated one day when the flamboyant young instructor who taught my senior courses in English and French, Eugene Fahnert, called me aside to ask if I had thought what else I might study in college apart from science. Not really, I confessed.

"You don't want your mind to become narrow, do you?" he asked.

"No, sir."

"Then make sure you sign up for some humanities courses every semester. Good solid ones you can get your teeth into. Literature, history, philosophy, art. That way, when you become a scientist, you'll know things that science can never teach you. And you'll hold on to the questions that science can't answer."

"Sounds like a good idea," I said.

"Would I have suggested a bad idea?" said Mr. Fahnert. "Just remember, don't ever give up your questions. Treasure them. Live them. Follow wherever they lead."

At the time I had not read Rilke, who gave the same advice to an aspiring poet in a famous little book, so I heard this call to cherish my questions coming from Mr. Fahnert alone, and that was authority enough. Of all my teachers in high school, he was the one who took the greatest joy in using his mind. He made learning seem as natural as breathing. It helped that he was young, still in his twenties, that he had served in the Army, had lived in Germany, had climbed mountains, that he skied and cooked and sang, and that he loved books. He was tall, athletic, wavy haired, with a defiant nose almost as big as my own, and he spoke English in a refined way that made it sound like an exotic language. While directing our school plays during the most fearful months of the Cold War, he would comment as freely on A-bombs or spies as he would on our acting. He convinced me that everything we do matters, that every hour can be charged with meaning, no matter how risky or bleak the world might seem.

Because of Mr. Fahnert, during that last year of high school I wrote down the questions that I used to lie awake wondering about. Here's the list:

How did the universe come to be?
What can we know of the power that sets everything moving?
How did life emerge from matter?
How did consciousness arise from life?
What is the role of mind in the universe?

How should we live?
What are the grounds for that "should"?
Why is there suffering?
Why are humans destructive and cruel?
Does anything of the self survive death?
What is our place in nature?
Do we have a purpose?
What is my true nature?
Where are we going?

I've held on stubbornly to those questions ever since—or perhaps they've held on to me. Although I don't expect to find conclusive answers, the search has taught me much of what I know.

The End of the World

In spite of the best efforts from Mr. Fahnert and other teachers who worked hard for their puny salaries, my rural high school was not a hotbed of learning. During my four years there, the greatest enthusiasm inspired by reading that I ever witnessed came when some boys in shop class discovered on the label of their wood glue a warning that dizziness might result from inhaling the vapors. The boys gave a cheer at this news and immediately began sniffing the glue. Afterward, they staggered down the hall arm-in-arm, kicking their legs high in a cancan and singing bawdy songs.

Most of my classmates planned on becoming farmers or secretaries, nurses or mechanics, tire builders, steelworkers, soldiers, or sales clerks. Few of us went on to college, and fewer still went to colleges more than a hundred miles from home. I had pretty much decided on going to Ohio State. But then in the winter of my senior year a basketball recruiter came to see me after one of our high-school games and urged me to apply to Brown University, in faraway Rhode Island, where they needed players like me. The sort of players they needed, I later realized, were ones who could pass Ivy League courses as well as Ivy League basketballs. I must have been the slowest point guard in Ohio ever to make a regional all-star team. Any college that needed me, I figured, must be hard up for talent. Still, I was flattered. So I applied, and to my surprise I was admitted, and to my even greater surprise Brown gave me a scholarship—not to play basketball, but to study physics.

I was fascinated by the way this ancient science joined beauty and terror. Even while physics was disclosing a vast, subtle, and magnificent universe, it was also unleashing awful powers. The splitting of atoms destroyed Hiroshima and Nagasaki shortly before I was born, and the headlines of my childhood were blackened by news of more and more lethal weapons. The Soviets launched their first sputnik when I was in seventh grade, which meant they could hurl a bomb at the arsenal if they chose.

Then in October of my senior year, aerial photos showed that the Soviets were placing missiles in Cuba, within easy reach of the United States. One night during a break in the dress rehearsal for a play, about a dozen of us huddled with Mr. Fahnert around a transistor radio in the school cafeteria and listened to President Kennedy warn the Soviet Union to remove those missiles or face grave consequences. My friends and I, sitting there in our costumes and greasepaint, knew that within a few days, even a few hours, everything we cared about could be blown away.

While the world held its breath over those missiles in Cuba, I turned seventeen, and on my birthday I went hiking through the October woods. Late in the afternoon I lay down on a ledge beside a creek, and I listened to the tumble of water and the fluster of birds, and I thought about war. I wondered if I would live to start college the next fall. I wondered if I would survive long enough to get married. I wondered if I would ever have children, and, supposing I did, what sort of world they would inherit.

Lying there beside the creek, gazing up through the scarlet haze of maples, I thought about what I should do with my life, however long or short it might be, whatever my talents might be. And I decided I would try to build things up instead of tearing them down; I would try to make discoveries and bring useful new gifts into the world, instead of consuming what was already here; I would work against cruelty and suffering; I would help make peace.

It was a teenager's vow, earnest and idealistic. The terms were too simple. I hadn't allowed for the world's ambiguities or the flaws in my own character. I hadn't allowed for the strength of hatred and greed. And yet, although I've often broken that vow, I've never renounced it. Without a sense of purpose, my life back then would have been hollow, and my life now would be aimless and idle. So I make stories, small gifts in return for the great gift of life.

Freshman

War wasn't the only trouble on my mind when I started college. All through high school the television carried images of black people struggling to gain their rights, along with images of white people trying to block their way. One side called for freedom with marches, sit-ins, boycotts, prayers, and speeches; the other side answered with clubs and bullets and ropes. Sheriffs turned whips and dogs on peaceful protesters. Black churches were bombed, homes were set on fire. Workers registering people to vote were killed, their bodies buried in an earthen dam. White mobs hurled stones and curses at black school children, who often found a politician or a posse barring the schoolhouse door.

Most of these ugly scenes played out in the South, where my father was from, where my grandparents and uncles and aunts and countless cousins lived, where I had been born. Later I would realize that no region of the United States and no social group has a monopoly on racism, but during those early years of the Civil Rights movement I felt ashamed of my southern birth and my white skin.

The week before I left for college, Martin Luther King Jr., delivered his "I Have a Dream" speech to hundreds of thousands of marchers in Washington. Phrases from that speech were ringing in my ears as I boarded a Greyhound bus for the long trip to Rhode Island. The dream of racial harmony, the dream of justice and a decent life for all people, seemed to me one worth living for. In order to serve that dream, I realized I would have to understand not merely nature but also human beings, and before I understood anyone else I would have to understand myself. By the time I reached the Greyhound station in Providence, forty hours after waving good-bye to my parents, I was eager to begin the work and scared I would fail. I was seventeen years old, skinny, shy, sun-roasted from building houses all summer, and painfully aware of my country upbringing.

I walked up a long steep hill from the bus depot to the university, lugging all my stuff in my grandfather's battered red sea chest. Every few minutes I had to stop and consult a map, for I had never seen the Brown campus, had never been within five hundred miles of Providence, had never been alone in any city. A taxi could have spared me some misery; but I knew nothing about taxis. During freshman orientation I would stumble on more and more things about which I knew nothing, and I would keep stumbling on new mysteries throughout my college years.

I did know how to read a map, however, so I found my way to the dorm, where I encountered one novelty after another. In the courtyard outside, two guys were playing catch with a blue plastic disk, about the size of a dinner plate. I had never seen such a gadget before, so elegant, so buoyant. Too shy to ask these strangers what it was, I would not learn until some time later that it was called a frisbee.

Rowdy music delivered with a strong British accent poured from an open window of the dormitory.

The music was new to me—but then nearly all music was new to me, since I had bought my first radio just the week before. I heard somebody yell, "Hey, turn up those Beagles," so I tucked away that bit of information, and later that first day I mentioned the name casually, to prove my sophistication, only to have another freshman say, "Not *Beagles,* you dope. *Beatles.*"

I found my room at the bottom of a stairwell, perfectly located so as to catch every noise in the dorm, and inside I found my roommate, who was taping up *Playboy* centerfolds on the wall over his bed. The pinups attracted a stream of visitors, all freshmen like us and all male, since the women were housed on a separate campus several blocks away and were allowed to visit men's dormitories only on Sunday afternoons. If a woman did choose to visit a man's room, we were instructed, the door had to be left open. How far open? Far enough to allow a matchbook to slip through. How thick a matchbook? Did the lights have to be on? Could the shades be drawn? The questions went on and on. They were not burning questions for me, since my only serious girlfriend was starting college a thousand miles away, at Indiana University. This Ruth McClure and I both came from families that made long-distance telephone calls only in emergencies, so we rarely spoke; but she wrote enchanting letters. Four years later we married, and we're still married.

Because my romantic energies were invested far away, I was able to form plainspoken friendships with a number of women in college, who, unlike the girls in high school, made no effort to hide their intelligence, passion, and wit. Trying to see through their eyes, I began to enlarge my own narrow vision. In the same way, I tried to reach in imagination across the gaps of religion or race or upbringing that separated me from my classmates.

Many of those classmates, male and female, seemed to know one another already, chatting about private schools they had attended, countries they had visited, Broadway plays they had seen, islands where they had cruised or mountains where they had skied. Their polish, their poise, their sense of belonging to this place made me feel like what I was, a rough kid from the back roads of Ohio, a scholarship boy, an outsider. While others seemed utterly confident of their right to be in a university, certain they would do well, I was not at all confident of belonging there. In fact, by the end of freshman week, I was beginning to worry that the scholarship committee had made a mistake. Perhaps my file had been confused with someone else's, someone truly qualified. I realize now that many of my fellow students were as unsure as I was; but at the time, I suspected that I was the only mistake, the only one likely to fail and be sent home in disgrace.

I had no intention of being sent home, in disgrace or otherwise, for the university seemed to me a gateway to the universe. Students were not gathered on every sidewalk discussing profound questions, as I had hoped. Indeed, some of them scorned thought and shunned work, as though the mind were made for cartoons and the body for beer. Fortunately, in every dorm and every class there were others who cared passionately about causes and ideas. I found these kindred spirits by listening for the intellectual buzz. I wanted to be part of that grand conversation, more than I had ever wanted anything.

So I worked hard. I studied as though my soul were at stake—as indeed it was. I dove into the life of the university. I joined clubs, went to concerts and soccer games and plays, watched films and ballets, listened to lectures by visiting dignitaries, sat at the feet of poets and novelists, marched in protests, visited nearby cities, toured museums, read omnivorously. Above all I listened and talked, as my friends and I explored the oldest questions of human existence and the latest issues of the day.

That fall, as men and women our own age were being shipped to Vietnam, my classmates and I began to feel the anguish of that war. In October, after much inner debate, I registered for the draft. In November, John Kennedy was assassinated, and we were shocked into recognizing that the social order, seemingly so firm, was in fact quite fragile. Within the first weeks of that semester I had to choose between science and sports, because physics lab was held at the same time as basketball practice. I chose science, which meant the world lost a slow point guard. The world did not gain a physicist, as it turned out, for I soon began to worry about the link between science and weapons, and I gave in to the tug of language.

When I look now at the journal I kept during my freshman year, and at the letters I sent to Ruth, I see a young man waking up, stretching his mind, brooding on the troubles of the world. The clumsy, earnest writer who appears in that journal did not think much about future jobs, but he thought constantly about vocation. What was he called to do? How should he use his new freedom? Scared and exhilarated at the beginning of college, that young man from the back roads of the Midwest would not only graduate but would go on to earn a Ph.D. in England, become a teacher, publish books. If someone had told me then that I would be sitting here now writing this account, and that strangers might read it, I would have laughed in disbelief. But here I am, laying down words.

Outsider

During four years at Brown, I proved that I belonged in an Ivy League university by taking the hardest courses and earning the highest grades, yet I never felt I belonged among my classmates. Many of them were rich, or at least their parents were; many scorned religion; most came from big cities on the east coast or the west; many were casual about alcohol and sex; most assumed that doors would be opened for them wherever they chose to go. I was a scholarship boy with just enough spending money to buy a sundae on Saturday night and a book every month or so. What little I understood about how to behave was bound up with the Bible and church. I came from the country—not the quaint back roads of New England, nor the tragic landscape of the deep South, nor the romantic spaces of the far West—but from clod-hopper country in the Midwest. I shunned alcohol because of the way it had tortured my father. While I knew a good deal about sex among farm animals, my knowledge of sex among humans was entirely theoretical. I took nothing for granted about my future. I knew that doors would open for me only if I shoved at them hard.

It was as though I spent four years wandering about in a grand reunion of someone else's family. The only way I could have felt more alien, without having come from overseas, would have been to wear dark skin. I don't pretend to know how it feels to be marked as an outsider by color, but I do know how it feels to linger on the margin, observing others who seem to belong by right of birth to a club that I can never join. Had I felt less of an outsider in college, I might not have become a writer. In those years I formed the habit of standing apart and watching how others behaved, not so as to imitate them, which I could not have done convincingly, but so as to be able to describe their gestures and manners in my journal. The challenge of turning experience into words, and the satisfaction from sometimes doing it well, began to rival for me the charm of physics.

Literature was also seducing me away from science. Following Mr. Fahnert's advice, I signed up each semester for an English class, reading Chaucer and Wordsworth and Poe. I saved up my small allowance to buy paperback volumes of Chekhov and Mann, Dostoevsky and Kafka, Yeats and Frost. In odd moments during the day and last thing at night before falling asleep, I read my way through lists of classics, from Aeschylus to Zola. By reading only durable books, I hoped to join an even grander conversation than the one in college from which I felt excluded.

Meanwhile, I was sending letters to Ruth in Indiana, describing for her what I had seen and done, commenting on my reading, pouring out my green thoughts. Between the letters and journals, I was writing five or ten pages a day, more than I have ever managed since. I told of solitary walks around Providence, the bricks luminous in sunlight or glimmering in lamplight or sleek with rain. I told of meeting beggars and bums, con men and drunks, told of glimpsing famous people on the stage of an auditorium, told how they moved and what they said, told of waiting for God beneath one or another of the city's tall white steeples. I wrote my way through shadowy tangles. I mapped the outlines of new continents and traced the edges of joy. The questions that haunted me, the ones I had written down during my last year in high school, kept rising onto the page. By turning my days into language, I laid hold of my life.

In letters to Ruth and in journals to myself, I described those rare moments when the bewildering world clicked into focus. There was the day when I paused outside Clark's Flower Shop on Thayer Street, near the Brown campus, and looked in through the window at a pot of red geraniums, flowers I had seen without excitement a thousand times in my growing up. But on this day the geraniums throbbed on their knotty stems, and I felt the urgency of their blossoms in my own veins, and for a moment the same pulse beat in all the fragrant flowers, in cars passing on the street, in dirt and buildings and sky and me, and that one pulse was the only reality.

And there was the day when I stood under an archway near the entrance of the student union, waiting for a break in the rain and talking with George Morgan, the professor who took most seriously my abiding questions. He was a mathematician and philosopher, a Jew who had fled from the Nazis as a child, moving with his family from Austria to Canada. He was my only teacher at Brown who listened carefully enough to hear the feelings behind my words. That day, as we stood watching the rain, at one point I spoke of myself lightly as a misfit.

"What do you mean?" Professor Morgan asked.

"Oh," I said, shrugging, "it's how I feel sometimes."

"Only sometimes?"

"Pretty often, I guess."

"Whether it's good or bad to be a misfit depends on what garment you're trying on," Professor Morgan said. Then he told me a story. Soon after his family reached Toronto, his mother took him shopping to buy a suit, so that he would look proper in this new place. In Vienna they would have gone to a tailor, but the family had left its money behind and could no longer afford handmade clothes. So they went to a store and he tried on ready-made suits. The clerk brought out one after another, but nothing fit. At length, exasperated, the clerk said to Mrs. Morgan, "Ma'am, I'm afraid your son's just the wrong size." Whereupon Mrs. Morgan drew herself up and announced, "My son is exactly the right size. It is your suits that do not fit."

"So you see," Professor Morgan concluded, "maybe you are no misfit. Maybe you're trying on the wrong clothes."

Foreigner

When I gave the valedictory address at my graduation, I wanted to repeat George Morgan's story, by way of explaining how I had come to accept being an outsider at Brown. But I thought it might offend those gathered in the First Baptist Church, there on the slope of the hill that I had climbed nearly four years earlier with my grandfather's sea trunk on my shoulder. So I spoke instead about the Vietnam War, civil rights, the nuclear arms race, the women's movement, threats to the environment, and poverty, and I told why the opinion of young people on these urgent issues deserved a hearing. How many listeners I offended anyway, I couldn't say, but the alumni magazine, which customarily printed the graduation address, chose not to publish mine.

I knew where I was headed next, because I had won a scholarship to Cambridge University, and I knew whom I would be traveling with, because I married Ruth later that summer, but when she and I rode the train north from London past crowded back gardens and brick warehouses and green velvet playing fields, I still didn't know for sure what I would be studying. I considered philosophy, history, and anthropology before I settled on literature. Although I would not have admitted it then to anyone, the truth was that I wanted to write, and I figured that reading fiction and poetry under the guidance of experts was the surest path to learning how.

During my first year at Cambridge I had the good fortune of being assigned for guidance to T. R. Henn, a bluff, burly Anglo-Irishman who had fought in the First World War and been imprisoned by the Japanese in the Second, and who at the time I knew him was nearing the end of a distinguished career. He still invited students to his home for teas, at one of which he introduced me to a young woman as a Golden Gloves boxing champion from Mississippi (a detail he'd picked up from a story I told about my father). After the introduction, Mr. Henn glanced at me with a merry hoist of his eyebrows before shuffling away. To my relief, the young woman announced that she detested boxing and then began talking about her research on graveyard imagery in Romantic poetry.

While interned by the Japanese, Mr. Henn had memorized the whole of Shakespeare and Yeats, along with the collected works of several lesser figures. When I knew him, a quarter century after the war, he could still recite entire plays and volumes of poems in a vibrant baritone. Every month or so he would host a literary evening in his rooms at the college. Perhaps a dozen students would gather in the candlelight to read from our own shaking manuscripts, and Mr. Henn would tell stories of meeting Yeats and O'Casey and other Irish worthies, and sometimes, after a glass or two of sherry, he would call up the ghosts of the writers he loved, and the candle flames would sway, and the words of the illustrious dead, though spoken by this man in our midst, would seem to come from the great beyond.

Each week during my first term at Cambridge, Mr. Henn assigned me a set of readings—all of

Euripides one week, all of Hopkins the next—and then I was to write in response an essay of ten or fifteen pages. I had no idea what an enormous labor he was imposing on me; whatever he expected, I was determined to do. I pounded out the essays on an ancient typewriter, three drafts, and then each Friday I showed up in Mr. Henn's dark, spacious, book-lined study to read the results aloud. As I read, he leaned back in his chair, eyes half-closed, hands resting on his ample belly, listening. As if to prove he was listening, every few minutes he would interrupt me to comment on a sentence, elaborate a point, or question me about one of my claims. Now and again, wishing to show me a pertinent quotation, he would rise grunting from his chair, limp over to the shelves and fetch down a book, which he would open to the exact page.

By the end of the fall term we had gone through this ritual eight times. After I read aloud my final essay, comparing the land as a character in *The Return of the Native* and *The Rainbow,* Mr. Henn paused longer than usual before making his final comment. "Mr. Sanders," he declared at last in his resonant voice, "you are wasting your time."

"I beg your pardon?"

"You know how to read, you know how to write. You should be pursuing your Ph.D. Why have you signed on for the B.A.?"

"That's what the scholarship officials told me to do. They say American universities never give adequate training in English."

"Then I beg to differ with the scholarship officials," Mr. Henn said. What I should do, he went on, was to choose a dissertation subject, draft a proposal, and submit it to the graduate committee. He would vouch for my training and ability. I felt jubilant. If this man who had known Yeats and memorized the whole of Shakespeare thought I was ready for graduate study, then I was ready. So I proposed to write a thesis on D. H. Lawrence, who fascinated me for reasons that I would only gradually recognize. The committee accepted the proposal and assigned me to my first choice of director, Raymond Williams.

Here was another cause for jubilation. Since my junior year at Brown, I had been reading Williams's books on culture and society and his accounts of growing up in the border country between England and Wales. Son of a railroad crossing guard, he was a working-class boy who had won scholarships to the best schools, including Cambridge, where he was first a student and then a don and then a professor. Through all that heady rise he kept his west country accent, his blue-collar sympathies, and his aloof stance as an outsider in the ranks of the privileged. I felt an obscure identification with him, as I did with Lawrence, and I relished the prospect of writing my dissertation under his direction.

Just as I was to begin work, however, Williams received an invitation to spend the following term at a university in Switzerland, and off he went. In what was supposed to have been a temporary arrangement, but which turned out to be permanent, the graduate committee reassigned me to a second director, a man who'd written a notable book on Lawrence. I learned from my fellow graduate students that this man had also been a prisoner of war in Asia, that he held the United States responsible for his hardships, and that he despised everything to do with America. When I called on him in his college rooms to seek his advice for my dissertation, before I could even say my name he declared, "England is an occupied country, you know."

"How is that, sir?" I asked in puzzlement.

"Occupied by your air force and your army and your millionaires."

"I'm afraid I don't—"

"First you wouldn't fight Hitler and Hirohito, and now you're killing peasants in Vietnam. You're using England as a staging area for your filthy war and as a playground for your bloody pilots. It's revolting." Having delivered his challenge, he crossed his arms and glared at me.

Instead of walking out, as I was tempted to do, I glared right back. At Brown I had felt apologetic for not fitting in, because there I was supposed to belong, but here in England I knew from the outset that I was a foreigner. I would not apologize for where I came from or who I was.

"I don't represent the American government," I told the professor. "I'm not a millionaire, and I hate the Vietnam War."

"Ah, so you've got some spunk," he said, brightening. "Well, then, tell me what you have in mind."

War and Peace

I had in mind a good deal more than I could have explained to that don at Cambridge who despised Americans. I wished not merely to write a dissertation about D. H. Lawrence, earn a Ph.D., and get a job. I wanted to discover my own path by trailing after this son of a hard-drinking, coal-mining father and an overbearing, pious mother; this scholarship boy from the back roads; this avid reader; this cross-country rambler and lover of flowers. I wanted to plumb the depths of his religious questioning, his shame and self-doubt. I wanted to understand how Lawrence had escaped from provincial backwardness to wander the world and make worthy books.

Nor could I have explained to that don my anguish over the war in Vietnam. When I'd first heard the name of that beleaguered country during my freshman year at Brown, I'd had to look it up on a globe; but now the shape of Vietnam was burned into my brain. Even in England, without a television, I came across images of the bloodshed and desolation almost every day. In my nightmares I watched villages burning, children seared by napalm wailing, forests withering from poison, body bags rising into the bellies of helicopters, tracer bullets slashing the sky. Here was the arsenal swollen to the size of a country. Here was the true paradise of bombs, a green and fertile land mauled by ingenious machines. In Vietnam, it seemed to me, the subtleties of science had been harnessed to the crude impulses of schoolyard bullies.

What could I do about this horror? I had marched against the war while a student in Providence, and now I was marching in Cambridge and London. I signed petitions. I wrote letters to Congress and the White House. Ruth and I joined with other Americans to help U.S. servicemen stationed in England put out a newsletter against the war, and for that the police trailed us through town as we rode our bicycles, agents showed up at our meetings and photographed our rallies, and detectives broke into our flat. No doubt they would have tapped our phone if we'd had one. We were such small fry that I could scarcely imagine what force the British and American authorities would have brought against those who truly threatened the war machine.

Meanwhile the machine ground on, spewing out corpses and blighting the Asian countryside and running up a heavy toll of ill will for the United States around the world. If I couldn't stop the juggernaut, at least I could refuse to climb on board. So I wrote from England to my draft board back home, telling them that I wished to register as a conscientious objector and that I was willing to perform alternative service, but that under no circumstances would I fight in Vietnam. They responded by classifying me I-A and instructing me to undergo a physical exam, in preparation for my being called into the army. There followed almost a year of heated correspondence between me and the draft board, they insisting that I serve my country, I insisting that I serve my conscience.

Adding yet another critical study of D. H. Lawrence to the hundreds already on the shelves seemed much less urgent a task than figuring out what I meant by conscience. If it was going to lead me into exile or jail, then I had better understand where the voice was coming from that told me to shun this war. Was it only the voice of cowardice? Was it the echo of scriptures, with their commandments to put away our swords and love our enemies? Was it the reverberation of those explosions at the ammunition dump in the arsenal? Was it the shudder from a childhood spent killing imaginary enemies? I had to understand my motives for refusing to fight if I was going to live with the consequences of that refusal.

I tried writing my way toward understanding, first in my journal, then in short stories, then in a clumsy, sprawling novel about a young man who chooses flight to Canada rather than add his hand to the slaughter in Vietnam. I thought less about becoming a writer than about saving my soul. Questions that had troubled me since childhood now became all the more pressing: How should we live, and what are the grounds for that "should"? What makes an action *wrong?* What gives an individual the right, even the obligation, to refuse the claims of his country? I read Tolstoy and Thoreau, Mahatma Gandhi and Martin Luther King Jr., Thomas Merton and Lao-Tzu, trying to clarify my beliefs. I began worshiping in Cambridge with the Society of Friends, the only religious group I could find that took seriously the gospel of peace. In the silence of meditation, I shrugged off much of my childhood faith like a shell outgrown, and I was left believing there is a power at the heart of things that wills life into being, a power that calls us to love one another and to honor all creatures, a power to which we are accountable. Although I no longer felt comfortable using the language of God, I could not shake the conviction that a divine presence informs the creation, from the wheeling stars to our own depths.

As my dispute with the draft board dragged on, Ruth and I began to talk of exile. When Lawrence and his German-born wife opposed that earlier war of 1914–18, their cottage in Cornwall was spied on by neighbors and staked out by police. He was arrested and interrogated, and eventually the two of them were forced to move away from the coast and to remain in the vicinity of London where they could easily be watched. Soon after the armistice, Lawrence fled his native country in disgust, and returned there for only a few brief visits during the rest of his life. Ruth and I decided that we might have to give up our own native country and stay in England, if we could get work permits; we might move to Canada, as the hero of my novel had done, to Sweden or France.

But the prospect of going years without seeing family and friends made me ache. I didn't know if I could bear to lose the fields and woods and thunderstorms of the Midwest, the dazzle of sycamores along the paths of creeks, the daily sound of American speech. Although Ruth would be able to go home for visits, my trouble would blight her life as well. So I petitioned for a hearing from my draft board, and they set a date months in the future. I prepared a long statement of my reasons for refusing to take part in this war. I arranged for a job as orderly in a charity hospital, in case the board agreed to let me perform alternative service.

"What if they turn you down?" Ruth asked.

"I still don't know."

"I'd rather live abroad than have you go to prison."

I remembered Thoreau spending a night in the Concord jail because he opposed America's assault on Mexico, King jailed in Birmingham because he marched for civil rights, Gandhi imprisoned in India for resisting British rule. As I wondered if I should follow their example, I thought of Ruth, thought of the shame my parents would feel, thought of surrendering books and typewriter and the open air, and I decided to choose exile.

But first I would do everything I could to prove the claims of my conscience. As the date for my hearing approached, I bought plane tickets for the trip home. I kept reading over my statement, adding new arguments, until I had it nearly memorized. Then the week before I was scheduled to depart, a letter arrived from the draft board announcing that they had reclassified me IV-F, a category reserved for those who are disqualified for military service by reason of physical or psychological or moral disabilities. They had washed their hands of me. They would find another young man to go in my place, a patriot, someone who didn't argue when his name was called.

Ever since that day I've carried in mind the man who went to Vietnam in my place. He may have died there, may have lost a limb; even if he survived the war and came home without scars, he would surely have lost his confidence in the sweetness of life. For the rest of my time in Cambridge I enjoyed the sweetness of life, and I enjoy it still, but I never forget the violence in us, the menace of our anger and fear. Nor do I forget the war that made me dig down to the foundations of conscience.

Teacher

Throughout our four years in England, the war burned on like an underground fire that nothing would put out, the smell of smoke and ash permeated everything, and it was burning still when Ruth and I sailed back to the country in whose name I had refused to fight. Near the docks in New York we rented a van from an office with steel bars over the windows and a Doberman chained to the counter. We loaded up our luggage, our bicycles, our crates of books, then headed for Indiana, Ruth's home state, where I would begin teaching at the university in Bloomington. When we crossed the Allegheny Mountains and rolled into Ohio, and I saw again the milky branches of sycamores blazing in creekbeds and heard cicadas and smelled fields of corn hot in the sun, I began to weep.

"What is it?" Ruth asked.

"I forgot how much I loved this place."

She gazed through the windshield at the rumpled landscape of Ohio, without asking me to explain what it was I loved or how I could have forgotten it. I had left the Midwest at age seventeen, laden with questions, and I was returning at age twenty-five, bearing academic degrees and even more questions. The degrees certified that I had mastered a subject called English, which nobody has ever been able to define, but I knew quite well that I had mastered nothing. I had read a few hundred books, yet all of them added together made up only a tiny fraction of those worth reading; I had learned how to write passable sentences;

I had published a few beginner's stories in British magazines; I had thought about my own small troubles and about the great troubles of the world. On such slender grounds, Indiana University had hired me to teach reading and writing to undergraduates, a fair proportion of whom were older than I was.

At Cambridge, doctoral students were not allowed to teach, so when I arrived in Bloomington I had never conducted a class. What little I knew about teaching had come from watching my own instructors over the years. While preparing for the semester, I recalled the best of them, the ones who had opened my eyes and ears and heart. Although distinct as individuals, each one impressive in his or her own way, these forceful teachers did have a few qualities in common: they enjoyed using their minds; they paid attention to what was going on outside the classroom; they were demanding and generous and patient; they cared passionately about learning; they lived in light of what they knew. They left their mark on me not merely because they passed on knowledge, although that was crucial, but because they demonstrated ways of being fully and richly human.

My students would quickly see—what an implausible phrase, "my students"—that I was a pretender, without much knowledge and with only the beginnings of a life to share. I figured they would be politically alert, restless with the routines of school, skeptical about the value of reading books while the world burned. They might stand up in the middle of my lectures to call for black power or women's rights;

they might shout demands for relevance as I spoke about the textures of words; they might walk out in disgust when I failed to show how literature could stop a war.

But the students who turned up for my classes that fall were dutiful and polite. They plowed through the volumes of Tolstoy and Melville and Lawrence that I asked them to read, and they struggled to write the weekly papers, and they puzzled over my gnarled comments when I gave the papers back. When I lectured, they scrawled in their notebooks. When I tried to get discussion going, they sensed that I had pages of notes to cover, and so they clammed up. When I asked them baffling questions, they stared at the ceiling or floor.

Midway through the fall semester I realized I was teaching with only part of myself, and that part was afraid. I feared silence in the classroom, feared the students' boredom or indifference, feared betraying my own ignorance. In defense, I filled the air with nervous talk. The only cure for fear, I decided, was to name it and face it. So at the next class meeting I told the students what I was feeling. First they looked nervously at one another, no doubt wondering if this young teacher had lost his grip, but as I went on to describe my own days in college, the questions that haunted me, my uncertainty about what to study or what to do with my life, gradually the students lowered their masks and began to speak.

"I thought professors had it all together," a woman said.

"I'm hardly a professor," I answered.

"You don't know everything there is to know about these books?" a man asked.

I laughed. "Not by a long sight."

"Like what Moby Dick stands for? Or why Anna throws herself under a train?"

"I've got my hunches," I said, "and I've read what a lot of other people think. But I don't know for sure. Nobody knows for sure. Not even Melville and Tolstoy."

"No wonder literature's so confusing," someone said.

"Just like life," another student remarked.

"Just like life," I agreed, "only books hold still so we can look at them."

After that exchange I felt less afraid. I kept making notes for discussion, but left them behind when I entered the classroom. I tried to ask only genuine questions, ones for which I had no certain answers. I learned to bear silence, realizing that it might cover the presence as well as the absence of thought. I allowed my enthusiasm as well as my ignorance to show. When I got worked up, as I often did, about a book or an idea or a cause, the students watched me with shy bemusement, and when I hushed they spoke up with passion of their own. The excitement in their voices gave me courage to keep on trying this difficult profession.

Father

The events that banished me from childhood were mostly public calamities—the Cuban missile crisis, the assassination of the Kennedy brothers and of Martin Luther King Jr., the police assault on student protesters at the 1968 Democratic convention, the race riots in American cities, the bombings on university campuses, the Vietnam War. The experiences that ushered me into adulthood were mostly private blessings—study at Brown, marriage to Ruth, life as a foreigner in England, apprenticeship as a teacher, the birth of my two children, and then, no blessing at all, the death of my father.

When my father arranged for me at the age of fifteen to hire on as a carpenter's helper for the summer, he said the hard work in the hot sun would make a man of me. But at the end of the summer, although I carried a few more dollars in my pocket and a few more pounds of muscle on my bones, I was just as callow as ever. Work alone would never make a man of me. Even the witnessing of public calamities would not make a man of me, so long as I viewed them from a distance, in bewilderment and dismay. So long as I didn't have to answer for what happened in the violent world, I could puzzle and grieve without growing up. True, the draft board forced me to answer for my convictions, yet as soon as they declared me unfit to serve, I could forget the war if I chose, or I could watch it once more from a safe remove.

What made me grow up was the taking on of responsibility for other people, intimately and inescapably, by becoming first a husband, then a teacher, then a father, then a householder and neighbor, and then, in a way I had not foreseen, by becoming fully a son. Any child must negotiate the demands of people older and stronger while pursuing its own desires, but adults must also meet the demands and the unspoken needs of those with whom they share house and workplace and neighborhood, those whom they lead or serve as well as those whom they love. When my own two children came along—Eva in my second year of teaching and Jesse four years later—I felt a jubilation unlike anything I had felt before, and I also felt an unprecedented obligation.

Ruth took on the hard labor of bearing each child, of course, and during their early years, while I struggled to become a teacher and writer, she took on most of their hour-by-hour care. But from the moment I saw the crown of Eva's head appear, slick and blue out of the womb, my life changed. Ruth laughed and cried as the baby surfaced, and through her hand clasped in mine I could feel her body pulsing with a strength so great that I was amazed the walls of the delivery room did not burst. I felt privileged to be there when Eva arrived, witnessing what my own father had not been allowed to see—the emergence of a brand-new child, vulnerable, dependent, and fierce with life. Eva's first breath made the air more precious. Her first cry tuned my ears to a fresh voice. When her eyes flickered open they brought the world into focus, shining onto each face and object in the room an unaccustomed light.

Within eight years of Eva's birth and within four years of Jesse's, my father died, a few months shy of sixty-five, his heart ruined by tobacco and alcohol. The drinking had soured my last few visits with him, for when I pleaded with him to stop, he answered me with bluster, lies, and grief. I had no idea what caused the grief, and if my father knew he would not say. On my final visit before his death, he and I went to cut up a fallen black walnut tree that a neighbor had said we could salvage. Jesse and Eva begged to go along, but I told them it would be too dangerous with the chain saw roaring and logs rolling. The truth was that I didn't want them to see my father's bloodshot eyes and trembling hands. He sensed the reason, and I could see that he felt angry and ashamed over being kept away from his grandchildren. He didn't trust himself to run the saw, so I did the cutting, and then the two of us wrestled the wood into the bed of his pickup.

As we sat on the tailgate resting between loads, he told me about his plans to have the walnut milled into boards, to cure the boards in his barn, and then to make wooden gifts for the family—tables, bookshelves, bowls, rocking chairs for the grandchildren, jewelry boxes for Mother and Sandra and Ruth. In the midst of the telling his voice broke, and I looked across to see the glisten of tears on his face, only the second or third time I had ever seen him cry. In the broken voice he said, "I don't mean to hurt my family, son."

"I know that, Dad."

"I just can't quit."

"We'll get you help."

"I've tried every cure there is, and nothing works."

"You're stronger than anything in a bottle," I insisted.

"No," he said, "I'm licked." And he stared at me with eyes so drained of hope that I flinched away.

Next morning, as Ruth and I were packing the car for our trip home, my father lay on the living room couch pretending to be a bear asleep while Jesse and

Eva crept up on him. When they drew near, suddenly he growled and wrapped them in his arms, nuzzling their gleeful faces with his raspy chin. How could anyone so vivid and strong simply give up? Surely he'd beat back the alcohol, I told myself. He'd live for years and years.

But he lived for just over a month. After the latest quarrel with my mother about his drinking, he left their retirement house in Mississippi for my brother's

place in Oklahoma, and there, early one cold morning, his heart burst. When I heard the news I swallowed my father's grief, without learning its source, and I took the taste of it into my mouth forever. I also took on responsibility for my mother, who soon moved into a house of her own in our town, and who lives there still, eighteen years after his death. Only in the years since his death have I understood how many more ways there are of failing than of succeeding as a husband, father, and son, and how inescapable are the claims of love.

Writer

My father didn't live to see what would become of all those pages that I typed out day after day, year after year, in dormitories and apartments and houses. Before he died, I had published a book derived from my dissertation on D. H. Lawrence, but that wasn't my real work, and I had published several dozen stories and essays in magazines, but they merely showed that I was an apprentice, learning my trade.

Why I had chosen the writing trade was a mystery to my father, and it remains largely a mystery to me. I never expected to earn a living from it. No teacher had ever urged me to it. No editor asked for my work. There were no writers in my family, none in the places where I grew up. I didn't meet a writer in the flesh until I was in college, and the few whom I did eventually meet while at Brown seemed arrogant or aloof. I've since come to understand that what struck me as arrogance or aloofness may only have been the armor they put on to defend themselves from the earnest attention of readers and would-be writers, like that younger version of myself. But at the time, I saw nothing in those writers to attract me, no glamour, no glint of wisdom, no shadowy depths.

I didn't take up the writer's trade because I wished to cut a certain figure in the world, nor because I wished to satisfy the adults who had charge of my education. I took up writing for the same reason a music-besotted youngster begins playing the piano or guitar—because I wanted to try my hand at the art that gave me such keen pleasure. I can't explain why I felt from the beginning such a passion for language, why I collected words, why I begged my sister to give me the secret of reading so soon after I had learned to talk. I can't explain why I worked my way through shelf after shelf of books at the library while hardly any of my childhood friends bothered to read. Nor can I explain why the making of stories opened paths for me through the dark woods of bewilderment, nor why, all these years later, it still seems to me such necessary work.

What I do know is that writing is my slow, stubborn way of asking questions, tracing the contours of feelings, thinking about what moves and troubles me. And I know that my impulse to write is bound up with my desire to salvage worthy moments from the river of time. Maybe all art is a hedge against loss. I realized quite early in childhood that I would die, that my parents and friends would die, that everyone I knew would pass away. But every child makes that discovery sooner or later. What pushed me beyond merely dreading those few private deaths was glimpsing in the arsenal the threat of wholesale death.

The land occupied by the arsenal had once been farms, and on my rambles I often came across the foundations of vanished houses and barns, fields and pastures grown up in thickets, fencerows gone wild. Before the land was farmed it had been forest, the hunting grounds for native people, and every arrowhead I found, every humped burial mound, was a reminder that entire nations could disappear. Inside those chain-link fences I stumbled on fields littered with the hulks of fighter planes from the last war, and parking lots crowded with howitzers and tanks for the next war. Most disturbing of all were the bunkers filled with explosives, for they made the very ground seem risky, and they kept me from forgetting the doomsday bombs, the ones powered by uranium and plutonium, which could wipe away in a blinding moment everything I loved. The arsenal convinced me that whatever time does not erode, we ourselves could destroy.

The circumstances of my childhood made life seem precarious, and therefore all the more precious.

Both feelings have stayed with me, and they color everything I write. By making up stories, I can't halt the erosive flow of time, can't protect what I cherish from the machinery of death, but I can enclose a small, orderly space, within which, for however brief a spell, meaning and beauty might endure. It's like building a dike against the pounding sea or a rampart against an invading army; even though you know the soldiers or the sea will eventually breach any barrier, for the moment you've created a place that is clear and safe. Since childhood, I've responded to the prospect of annihilation by writing down what I think, what I feel, what I take in through my senses, what I remember and imagine. I enter the country of language not to escape the chancy world that precedes and surrounds all language, but to ponder that world, to hold up portions of it for examination, to decipher its patterns and celebrate its wonders.

For a long while, nobody except my family knew that I was writing, and for an even longer while hardly anybody else cared, and for good reason. I learned the craft slowly, privately, without guidance from fellow apprentices, without any teachers aside from those I found in books. Although I wrote steadily for a decade after becoming a teacher myself, I had little to show for it except piles of manuscripts and a clutch of magazines bearing my name on the contents page. On such slim evidence I would not have called myself a writer. I was merely a person who wrote, along with countless others in every city and town and village in the land. The boxes full of typescript were like houses which no one but the carpenter had ever entered.

Although I questioned my skill, my vision, even at times my sanity, I cared too much about writing to quit. I kept filling those boxes, and gradually I learned how to build houses of words that others might want to visit.

My father had been dead for two years when *Wilderness Plots* came out, my first real book. A photograph in my study shows me signing the first copy, with Eva and Jesse looking on. Eva was ten that summer and Jesse six. From the time they could crawl, they had been turned away from my shut door, had been asked to do without my company for the morning hours, because I was writing. And what was the point of all that writing? Here at last, in a slender volume the color of whole wheat flour, was evidence that my solitary work had not been merely selfish, that the hours had not been wasted.

Over the next three years, seven more of my books appeared, novels and story collections and nonfiction narratives. A few magazines began publishing my work regularly, a few editors began asking to see anything I had on hand, a few colleges began inviting me to visit. When I stood before audiences and read aloud the words that I had set down in solitude, I felt less guilty for having locked myself away hour after hour, year after year, from family and friends and the open air. What I had made for so long in private was finally being taken up in the hands and minds of strangers. My reports of insight and memory and affection, the most frail and fleeting of things, had become durable through being shared.

Scott Russell Sanders

A PORTRAIT

by Scott Slovic

The reward for living an attentive life is life itself. One gets the sense, reading the work of Scott Russell Sanders, that scarcely a sliver of experience escapes his notice, his rumination, and his eventual analysis and interpretation by way of story. Time functions in Sanders's work not as a dispersing force, an entropic process of loss and dissolution, but rather as a flexible medium in which the writer's memory can do its work, spreading out moments of experience like specimens on a biologist's slide, adjusting the light just right, pushing the description and explanation to the point of revelation, and skipping to the next slide. This is the process, the structure, of the preceding series of autobiographical essays.

Can you imagine the mind of this writer not deriving meaning from any kind of experience? In the chapter called "Writer," Sanders recalls that he never met an author "in the flesh" until his undergraduate years at Brown University, and then found these people "arrogant or aloof," perhaps because of the armor they constructed to fend off over-earnest attention from readers. Sanders himself, though,

89

seems incapable of such relationships with his audiences, with the world. Or, to put it better, he seeks out postures of openness and innocence toward the world, opportunities for direct contact and understanding. It's hard to show this any better than simply to point to the opening chapter of this *Credo* volume, "The Gift." Sanders's ideal audience, in a sense, is a group of children, put at ease by the speaker's own silly humanity, his hammed-up costume or his self-confessed foibles. When the audience drops its pretensions, its defenses, the author, too, speaks as plainly and directly as possible, seeking to produce a story—a realm of "clear light"—in which it becomes possible to glimpse "some remarkable person, some worthy gesture, some wild creature."

The actual presentation of a story to an audience, whether physically present listeners or imagined readers, becomes a process of exploration and interpretation for this writer. And any gifts offered by the writer are multiply reciprocated in the attentiveness of the audience. Thus the story of the Cincinnati schoolboy named Charles who exchanges an arrowhead for a story serves as both a concrete, matter-of-fact encounter and a parable for the writer's engagement with the world. Life is a series of encounters which offer opportunities for the exchange of gifts. "Gifts" may be physical objects, but their value is imagined— the value of a gift is generated by the minds of giver and receiver. Whether railing against the flooding of his childhood home or celebrating the common joys of baking bread with family and neighbors, Sanders's tales of mundane experience expand with meaning, with a sense of values. "Issues" assume the form of tangible stories, and stories, in turn, trigger readers' imaginations. Walk out into the world after reading these crisp, unassuming narratives, and your own life seems more real.

Some readers might look askance at an author pre-occupied with the ordinary, the commonplace. But this is Sanders's territory, and he has mastered the craft of telling stories of the commonplace in book after book during the past two decades. He not only celebrates what is common, but is defiant about it. In an essay called "The Common Life," collected in the 1995 volume *Writing from the Center,* he asserts:

> In our common life we may find the strength not merely to carry on in the face of the world's bad news, but to resist cruelty and waste. I speak of it as common because it is ordinary, because we make it together, because it binds us through time to the rest of humanity and through our bodies to the rest of nature. By honoring this common life, nurturing it, carrying it steadily in mind, we might renew our households and neighborhoods and cities, and in doing so might redeem our-selves from the bleakness of private lives spent in frenzied pursuit of sensation and wealth.

Family, neighbors, humble processes of preparing meals and repairing an old house, familiar and undra-matic landscapes—these elements provide the subtle texture of Scott Russell Sanders's life and writing. Newcomers to the genre of nature writing may wonder why Sanders's work contains so many people, is set so frequently in the farmlands and small towns of the Midwest rather than in sublimely wild places, and so often self-consciously examines language itself. Is this "nature writing" at all? Or is Sanders's work something broader and perhaps deeper than this familiar term suggests? Life writing—or community writing.

Sanders received the prestigious Associated Writing Programs Award for Creative Nonfiction in 1987 for his second book of essays, *The Paradise of Bombs*. In the introduction to this book, he states that essays are his "efforts at remembering where we truly live—not inside a skull, a house, a town or nation, not inside any human creation at all, but in *the* creation." By working through his direct relationships with sensory things—animals, plants, people, tools, language—Sanders seeks to understand how the world works and how his own connection to the world constantly torques and shifts. The process of coming to terms with the world, and with one's relationship to it, is endless and always new. Just as Loren Eiseley, one of the founders of the modern American nature essay with such books as *The Immense Journey* and *The Unexpected Universe* in the 1950s and 1960s, spent his entire literary career asking and re-asking the same basic questions about the place of the self amidst the vast genetic process of evolution, Sanders finds himself scrutinizing in story after story the workings of his senses, his daily environment in late twentieth-century America, his feelings of attachment and abhorrence—the emotional physics of human experience.

"I find myself brooding in essay after essay," he writes,

> on the origins of violence, especially that collective madness we call war; on the ways we inhabit the land; on our fellowship with animals; on the use of hands; on the tangled legacy of maleness; on the mysterious gravitation of love. But such an abstract listing of themes is misleading, for the essays themselves deal only in the concrete and particular. They are narratives; they speak about the world in stories, in terms of human actions and speech and the tangible world we inhabit.

This passage, although addressing the scope and method of *The Paradise of Bombs* in particular, goes a long way toward illuminating the entirety of Sanders's work as a writer, above all emphasizing his devotion to the *tangible*—the "concrete and particular" object or creature or place or happening or phrase. This is both the technique and the objective of his stories, his fiction as well as his nonfiction. His 1985 novel, *Terrarium,* explores the implications of a nightmare existence where characters are removed from the physical world of nature and prohibited by new taboos from having physical contact with other human beings; it is a story in which the cautious resolution combines a return to wild nature with the renewed acceptance of senses. The pursuit of tangible experience is one of the abiding motifs of Sanders's work. In a 1997 interview, he explained the scene from his essay "Earth's Body" (collected in the book *Staying Put)* where he wanders out into his backyard and hugs a tree:

> I confess that I do hug trees, in my backyard and anyplace else where I happen to meet impressive ones. I hum beside creeks, hoot back at owls, lick rocks, smell flowers, rub my hands over the grain in wood. I'm well aware that such behavior makes me seem weird in the eyes of people who've become disconnected from the earth. But in the long evolutionary perspective, they're the anomaly. Our bodies were made for this glorious planet, tuned to its every sound and shape. . . .

For Sanders, literature that neglects our animal selves, that never explores beyond the limited human realm, is "false" and even "pathological." The primary goal of any writer who "sees the world in ecological perspective," he wrote in a 1987 essay called "Speaking a Word for Nature" (later collected in *Secrets of the Universe),* is "how, despite the perfection of our technological boxes, to make us feel the ache and tug of that organic web passing through us, how to *situate* the lives of characters—and therefore of readers—in nature." Ironically, the tool writers use to inspire this renewed sense of our own physicality, and the tool readers must rely upon to appreciate this message, is imagination. "How we inhabit the planet," Sanders explains in the concluding paragraph of the same essay, "is intimately connected to how we imagine the land and its creatures." It is, of course, the traditional role of literature to help us imagine, and reimagine, ourselves and the world.

In addition to this fascination with sensual experience, with tangibility, other primary dimensions of Sanders's work—goals of his writing that are indiscernible from its form—include clarity, accessibility, and candor. Readers will recall how Henry David Thoreau offered an apology on the opening page of *Walden* for writing in the first person:

> I should not talk so much about myself if there were any body else whom I knew as well. Unfortunately, I am confined to this theme by the narrowness of my experience.

And then Thoreau proceeded to write in what most contemporary readers are likely to consider a curiously elliptical, self-effacing style. Not so Sanders. The self is everywhere in his work, especially in his nonfiction—and at the same time nowhere. To be sure, his essays inevitably cohere around personal narratives, stories rooted in actual experiences. And yet, as the author explains in various essays and introductions, "I write of my own life only when it seems to have a larger bearing on the lives of others. . . . I write in a personal voice about the impersonal, the not-me, for the world is a larger and more interesting place than my ego."

The use of personal experience as the basis for

story and reflection is a technique essential to making ideas tangible and real—accessible to the reader, who can in turn substitute him- or herself for the speaker in these quotidian tales. But Sanders argues further that the essay is, for him, a realm of sincerity and candor: "In the essay, you had better speak from a region pretty close to the heart or the reader will detect the wind of phoniness whistling through your hollow phrases." In a 1997 essay for the *Chronicle of Higher Education* called "From Anonymous, Evasive Prose to Writing with Passion," he recalls his own apprenticeship as an academic writer:

> I learned to write clean, clear sentences, when lucidity was called for, but I also learned to write sentences so murky that even a veteran grammarian could not have diagrammed them. When I was uncertain of my ground, or merely bored, I could always hide in the verbal thickets and dare the reader to track me down. I learned how to camouflage my own views behind those of the authorities I quoted. During my long apprenticeship in school, I mastered the anonymous prose that mumbles like elevator music in the background of our industrial civilization— the prose of memos, quarterly reports, grant proposals, program summaries, newscasts, run-of-the-mill journalism, court briefs, perfunctory scholarship, and tidy English papers.

The point of this essay is to recant this typical form of academic prose and to call for new passion and clarity and responsibility in writing and in the teaching of writing. Recalling his own experiences as a writing teacher, Sanders acknowledges the difficulty of re-forming the kinds of discourse that have become commonplace in our society, the difficulty of compelling students to stop thinking of writing as "a game played with hollow figures lined up on a blank field, abstract and safe" and instead to "climb onto the page and risk their own necks." The reader need look no further than Sanders's own work—almost any example will do—to see the risks and especially the benefits of clear, direct expression and accessible, down-to-earth material.

What it all boils down to—this writing life—is the issue of responsibility. For Sanders and writers like him, from Barry Lopez to Wendell Berry, literary expression emerges from experience and returns to the world, if successful, by changing or intensifying readers' worldviews and affecting daily behavior. "Unless we are willing to quit holding individuals accountable for their actions," he writes, "we should hold them accountable for their words." This is clearly the code by which Sanders himself lives and writes. A few years ago, Sanders and his friends Alison Deming and Richard Nelson expressed this idea of the writer's responsibility to the world in a rather profound and direct way. The three of them, all regular contributors to the important environmental magazine *Orion,* composed a letter to *Orion* readers, calling for an "Ecological Bill of Rights and Responsibilities." "Recently, the three of us were slopping our way through the rain in a forest near Sitka, Alaska, talking about the fate of the earth, sharing our grief and dismay," the letter begins.

> We are friends drawn together by a shared passion for wildness and words. For thirty or forty years, we have been learning all we can about nature, through science and literature, through the stories of indigenous peoples and our own explorations; and for the past twenty years we have been writing books to say what we've discovered and why it matters. Our work as writers, we have come to realize, is not enough to protect the things we love.

Although these writers are among the liveliest storytellers and most lyrical crafters of imagery currently working in the English language, their aim—their self-imposed obligation—is "to give more political force to [their] concern for the earth." They confess at one point: "Words on a page do not accomplish anything by themselves; but words taken to heart, words carried in mind, may lead to action."

Scott Russell Sanders came by his sense of responsibility and necessity—responsibility to other people and to particular places of the heart; the necessity of living a humble, hands-on life—quite naturally. His mother, Eva Mary Solomon, was born to an immigrant doctor in Chicago; his father, Greeley Ray Sanders, came from a family of cotton farmers in Mississippi. After their first child, Sandra, was born in Chicago in 1942, the Sanders family spent the rest of World War II in Mississippi, where Scott's father worked at Gulf Ordnance Plant, loading shells. The family moved to Memphis, Tennessee, in 1945, and Scott was born that year on October 26. His father made tires at Firestone, eventually becoming a supervisor. For five years, the family lived across the road from a farm operated by black inmates from the local prison. Their neighbors were an elderly black couple on one side, a white farming family on the other.

From 1951 to 1956, they lived at Ravenna Arsenal in Portage County, Ohio—this place later became the subject of the title essay in *The Paradise of Bombs*. Scott's brother Glenn was born in 1954. Two years later, the family moved to a farm in Charlestown township, close to the Ravenna Arsenal. The Soviet Union launched its first sputnik in the fall of 1957, an important event for twelve-year-old Scott, as this in turn launched a heightened interest in the natural sciences in American schools. In 1963, the same year Scott graduated from Southeast High School in Portage County, work began on a dam for West Branch Reservoir, which eventually flooded the woods and fields near the Sanders family farm that had been Scott's childhood universe. Years later, as he recounts in the opening chapter of *Staying Put,* the author returned to survey the reservoir, only to feel "truly exiled." "One's native ground," he reflected,

> is the place where, since before you had words
> for such knowledge, you have known the

smells, the seasons, the birds and beasts, the human voices, the houses, the ways of working, the lay of the land, and the quality of light. It is the landscape you learn before you retreat inside the illusion of your skin. . . . Even if you move to the antipodes, even if you become intimate with new landscapes, you still bear the impression of that first ground.

His family moved to Lake Charles, Louisiana, the year he finished high school, and Scott left home to study physics at Brown University on an Alfred P. Sloan Scholarship.

At Brown, he spent three years as a physics major before switching to literature. "Fear of failing," he later recalled, kept him working so hard that he graduated summa cum laude and valedictorian. But he never shed the "sense of being an outsider, a hick among sophisticates"—and, thus marginalized from his aristocratic and worldly classmates, he "formed the habit of looking and listening" which would later serve him so well as a writer. In August of 1967, Scott married Ruth Ann McClure, whom he had met several years earlier during a high-school science camp. Supported by a Marshall Scholarship, a Danforth Fellowship, and a Woodrow Wilson Fellowship, he attended graduate school in English at Cambridge University from 1967 to 1971. Although he ended up writing a scholarly dissertation on D. H. Lawrence, he also drafted some of the short stories during this time that would eventually appear in his collection *Fetching the Dead* (1984).

Sanders returned to the United States in 1971 to begin a teaching job at Indiana University, a position he continues to hold today. In 1973, when their daughter Eva was born, the Sanderses moved into the house where they still live and which Scott describes in detail in many of his essays. His first book, *D. H. Lawrence: The World of the Major Novels,* was based on his Cambridge dissertation and appeared in 1974. After a stint as a writer-in-residence at Phillips Exeter Academy in New Hampshire in 1974–75, Scott returned to Indiana University and began writing science fiction stories. Following the birth of their son Jesse in 1977, the Sanders family spent 1978–79 on sabbatical leave in Eugene, Oregon, and it was there that Scott finished two books of fiction, *Bad Man Ballad* and *Wilderness Plots,* began writing the futuristic novel *Terrarium,* and produced a number of the essays that would eventually be collected in *The Paradise of Bombs.*

Wilderness Plots was accepted for publication in 1982, nearly a decade after the publication of Sanders's first book. Since then, he has published a steady stream of books, currently including seven books for children, eight novels and collections of short stories, and nine books of essays and literary nonfiction. A National Endowment for the Arts Fellowship in 1983–84 enabled him to write *Stone Country* and *Hear the Wind Blow* and to begin a novel on the life of John James Audubon, part of which appeared in 1984 as *Wonders Hidden: Audubon's Early Years,* published in a special edition by Capra Press, together with Ursula K. Le Guin's *The Visionary: The Life Story of Flicker of the Serpentine*. Sanders describes his friendship with Charles and Ursula Le Guin in the 1995 afterword to the second edition of *Terrarium,* explaining that the house of one of the book's central characters is loosely modeled after the Le Guins'.

With the aid of a Lilly Endowment Fellowship, Sanders spent 1986–87 at M.I.T., where he wrote the novels *The Engineer of Beasts* and *The Invisible Company,* as well as the first of the essays that would later become *Secrets of the Universe. The Paradise of Bombs* received the 1987 Associated Writing Programs Award for Creative Nonfiction, leading to an eventual string of major literary awards that would include a PEN Syndicated Fiction Award in 1988, a Lannan Literary Award in 1995, and a Great Lakes Book Award in 1996, among others. The publication of *Secrets of the Universe* in 1991 began Sanders's long-term association with Boston's Beacon Press that would help to make the press a central institution in the late twentieth-century renaissance of American nature writing; as of now, five of his books have been published (or republished) by Beacon.

A Guggenheim Fellowship in 1992–93 enabled Sanders to finish *Staying Put* and two children's books, *Here Comes the Mystery Man* and *The Floating House.* The following year, he completed yet another essay collection, *Writing from the Center,* as well as the children's book, *A Place Called Freedom.* In addition to his important (and prodigiously productive) work as a writer, Sanders has been recognized as a superb teacher at Indiana University with such honors as the Frederick Bachman Lieber Award for Distinguished Teaching (1992) and the Students' Choice Teaching Award (1998). In 1995, he received the College of Arts and Sciences Alumni Association Distinguished Faculty Award at Indiana.

In June of 1995, Sanders delivered one of the featured readings at the first international conference of the Association for the Study of Literature and Environment at Colorado State University in Fort Collins, after which he and his son Jesse went hiking for several days in the nearby Rocky Mountains. This hiking trip, and the father-son conflict that occurred on the trail, inspired what may, in the long run, turn out to be one of Sanders's most important projects, the nonfiction book called *Hunting for Hope: A Father's Journeys* (1998), which explores in microcosm the tendency of environmental literature to emphasize humanity's role in degrading the planet without necessarily offering tenable solutions to this process, this historical trend.

In the afterword to the second edition of the speculative novel *Terrarium,* Sanders recalls his struggles with despair while trying to complete the narrative in the early 1980s:

> The novel was on my mind in the afternoons as I roamed with the children, and the children were on my mind in the mornings as I wrestled with the novel. Jesse and Eva tugged my thoughts into the future. What sort of earth

would they inherit? Would they suffer from nuclear war? From pollution? From hunger? When they were my age, would they be able to breathe the air or drink the water? Would they have confidence enough to bear their own children? If so, would those children still be able to see whales or wolves? Would they meet any wildness at all?

This rhetorical mode of critique and complaint and dismay recurs throughout Sanders's work—it is just as common in these stories as the language of revelation and celebration. We find it in "The Singular First Person" when the author laments that, "Like the blandburgers served in their millions along our highways, most language served up in public these days is textureless, tasteless mush." This frustration with modern American language is echoed several years later in the essay "Beneath the Smooth Skin of America," when he argues, "America is still a manifold and textured land, nor could any human force ever wear it down to utter uniformity; but each year it is rubbed a bit smoother by technology and commerce, by the media, and by our feverish mobility." The price of perception, of awareness, it appears, is the compulsion to worry—to notice loss and degradation, to rail against it, and to sense the futility of one's efforts.

That Sanders is sensitive to the limits of his own occasionally jeremiadic language is revealed in the concluding chapter of *Staying Put*, "Telling the Holy," which offers the story of one Jeremiah Lofts, a neighbor of the Sanders family when Scott was nine or ten years old, who predicted the end of the world and then "never showed his face in public again" when the prediction failed to come true. The importance of stories in our culture, in all cultures, Sanders goes on to suggest, is not that these stories reveal indisputable, final truth, but that they probe the holiness and mysteriousness of the universe, that they help us begin to see "where we are, how others have lived here, how we ourselves should live."

In his most recent book, *Hunting for Hope,* Sanders further investigates the darkness of his own vision, his own language, responding to the profound challenge issued by his son during the stressful 1995 trip they took together to the Colorado Rockies. After a day of brooding and silence on the trail, Jesse expresses his frustration with his dad:

> Your view of things is totally dark. It bums me out. You make me feel the planet's dying and people are to blame and nothing can be done about it. There's no room for hope. Maybe you can get by without hope, but I can't. I've got a lot of living still to do. I have to believe there's a way we can get out of this mess. Otherwise, what's the point?

"There was too much truth and too much hurt in what he said for me to fire back an answer," Sanders realizes. "Had I really deprived my son of hope?" This is, of course, one of the fundamental questions concerning the entirety of Sanders's work, and concerning the very genre of contemporary environmental

literature. Is this merely a form of hyperbolic, apoca-
lyptic ranting or are there some practical, inspiring
messages in this literature that we as readers can take
to give us "courage for the journey"? Without deny-
ing the challenges we face in the modern world,
challenges that show few signs of abating, Sanders
points to the small beauties of the world and to the
achievable transformations of lifestyle that might
offer us solace and some chance of sustainability.
Here, in "The Country of Language," in the literature
of landscape and community, we find despair and
hope, bleakness and beauty, inevitably intertwined.
Stories cannot offer instant solutions to our prob-
lems, but they can fill the journey, the struggle, with
meaning.

Bibliography of Scott Russell Sanders's Work

by Scott Slovic

BOOKS

Hunting for Hope. Boston: Beacon Press, 1998.

Writing from the Center. Bloomington: Indiana University Press, 1995.

Staying Put: Making a Home in a Restless World. Boston: Beacon Press, 1993.

Secrets of the Universe. Boston: Beacon Press, 1991.

In Limestone Country. Revised edition of *Stone Country*, Boston: Beacon Press, 1991.

The Invisible Company. New York: Tor Books, 1989.

The Engineer of Beasts. New York: Orchard Books/ Franklin Watts, 1988.

The Paradise of Bombs. Athens: University of Georgia Press, 1987. New York: Simon & Schuster, 1988 (paperback edition). Boston: Beacon Press, 1993 (paperback edition).

Audubon Reader: The Best Writings of John James Audubon. Bloomington: Indiana University Press, 1986. Tokyo: JIIC, 1994 (Japanese edition).

Bad Man Ballad. New York: Bradbury/Macmillan, 1986.

Hear the Wind Blow. New York: Bradbury/Macmillan, 1985.

Stone Country. With photographs by Jeffrey A. Wolin. Bloomington: Indiana University Press, 1985.

Terrarium. New York: Tor Books, 1985. Bloomington: Indiana University Press, 1995 (with new afterword).

Fetching the Dead. Champaign: University of Illinois Press, 1984.

Wonders Hidden: Audubon's Early Years. Santa Barbara: Capra Press, 1984.

Wilderness Plots: Tales about the Settlement of the American Land. New York: Morrow, 1983. Columbus: Ohio State University Press, 1988 (paperback edition).

D. H. Lawrence: The World of the Major Novels. London: Vision Press, 1974. New York: Viking, 1974 (U.S. edition).

STORYBOOKS FOR CHILDREN

Crawdad Creek. Washington, D.C.: National Geographic, 1999.

Meeting Trees. Washington, D.C.: National Geographic, 1997.

A Place Called Freedom. New York: Atheneum, 1997.

The Floating House. New York: Macmillan, 1995.

Here Comes the Mystery Man. New York: Bradbury/ Macmillan, 1994.

Warm as Wool. New York: Bradbury/Macmillan, 1992.

Aurora Means Dawn. New York: Bradbury/Macmillan, 1989. In *La vide en nuestro mundo,* edited by

Richard G. Boehm, et al. New York: Harcourt
Brace, 1997 (Spanish translation).

UNCOLLECTED STORIES

"The Wilds." *Potlatch* (1994).

"July Snow." *Hopewell Review* 5 (1993).

"Harm's Reach." *Voices Louder Than Words: A Second
Collection,* edited by William Shore. New York:
Vintage, 1991.

"Dancing in Dreamtime." *Omni* 13, no. 1 (October
1990).

"Dance." *Arts Indiana* (August 1990).

"The Fossil." *Beloit Fiction Journal* 5, no. 2 (Spring
1990).

"A Gordon Milk Suite." *Gettysburg Review* 1, no. 4
(Autumn 1988).

"Travels in the Interior." *Omni* 8, no. 3 (December
1985). *Omni* Japanese Edition (October 1986,
Japanese translation).

"Tree of Dreams." *Isaac Asimov's Science Fiction
Magazine* 9, no. 5 (May 1985).

"Ascension." *Isaac Asimov's Science Fiction Magazine*
9, no. 2 (February 1985).

"The First Journey of Jason Moss." *Poet & Critic* 16,
no. 2 (Winter 1985).

"Quarantine." *Habitats,* edited by Susan Shwartz.
New York: Daw Books, 1984.

"The Circus Animals' Desertion." *Omni* 6, no. 3
(December 1983). *Omni* Japanese Edition (June
1985, Japanese translation).

"The Artist of Hunger." *Isaac Asimov's Science Fiction
Magazine* 7, no. 7 (July 1983).

"Wake." *Indiana Review* 6, no. 3 (Summer 1983).

"Land Where Songtrees Grow." *Magazine of Fantasy and Science Fiction* 63, no. 3 (September 1982).

"Mountains of Memory." *Isaac Asimov's Science Fiction Magazine* 6, no. 9 (September 1982).

"The Audubon Effect." *Omni* 4, no. 6 (March 1982). *Omni* Japanese Edition (July 1987, Japanese translation).

"The Sleepwalker." *Magazine of Fantasy and Science Fiction* 61, no. 6 (December 1981).

"The Anatomy Lesson." *Isaac Asimov's Science Fiction Magazine* 5, no. 11 (October 1981).

"The Recovery of Vision." *North American Review* 266, no. 1 (March 1981).

"The Eros Passage." *New Dimensions Eleven,* edited by Robert Silverberg and Marta Randall. New York: Pocket, 1980.

"Touch the Earth." *Edges,* edited by Ursula K. Le Guin and Virginia Kidd. New York: Pocket, 1980. "Berührt die Erde." *Kanten,* edited by Ursula K. Le Guin and Virginia Kidd. Munich: Wilhelm Heyne Verlag, 1983 (German translation).

"The History of Fiction." *Tracks* 7, no. 2 (Spring 1979).

"Hunt." *Minnesota Review,* new series, no. 7 (Fall 1976).

"Bus South." *Transatlantic Review* 33/34 (1969).

"The Operation." *Cambridge Review* (February 1968).

UNCOLLECTED ESSAYS AND CRITICISM

"Heartwood." *Natural Home* (May/June 1999).

"Teaching Thoughtful Students the Rudiments of Hope." *Chronicle of Higher Education* (April 9, 1999).

"Lessons from the Land Institute." *Audubon* (March/April 1999).

"Dos razones por las que siempre necessitamos una buena historia." Spanish translation of "The Most Human Art." *Integral* (Barcelona) 219 (March 1998).

"To Eva, on Your Marriage." *Fathering Daughters: Reflections by Men,* edited by Dewitt Henry and James Alan McPherson. Boston: Beacon Press, 1998.

"From Anonymous, Evasive Prose to Writing with Passion." *Chronicle of Higher Education* (October 10, 1997).

"Witnessing to a Shared World." *A View from the Loft* 19, no. 9 (April 1997).

"The Power of Stories." *Georgia Review* 51, no. 1 (Spring 1997).

"Reaching Through My Hands." *Notre Dame Magazine* 26, no. 1 (Spring 1997).

"Silence." *Witness* 11, no. 2 (1997).

"Sous la peau lisse de l'Amerique." French translation of "Beneath the Smooth Skin of America." *Interculture* (Quebec) 29, no. 2 (Summer/Fall 1996).

"Making a Reader's House Fit a Home." *Boston Sunday Globe* (December 17, 1995).

"Honoring Good Work." *Orion Society Notebook* 1, no. 2 (Autumn/Winter 1995).

"Amos and James." *Shenandoah* 45, no. 3 (Fall 1995).

"Stepping Out." *Brown Alumni Monthly* 95, no. 9 (July 1995).

"On the Trail of Books." *Arts Indiana* 17, no. 5 (Summer 1995).

"Wendell Berry." An interview conducted together with Carol Polsgrove. *The Progressive* (May 1990).

"Death of a Homeless Man." *The Progressive* 51, no. 3 (March 1987).

"Lady Chatterley's Loving and the Annihilation Impulse." *D. H. Lawrence's "Lady": A New Look at "Lady Chatterley's Lover,"* edited by Michael Squires and Dennis Jackson. Athens: University of Georgia Press, 1985.

"D. H. Lawrence and the Resacralization of Nature." *D. H. Lawrence: The Man Who Lived,* edited by Robert B. Partlow and Harry T. Moore. Carbondale: Southern Illinois University Press, 1981.

"Women As Nature in Science Fiction." *Future Females: A Critical Anthology,* edited by Marleen Barr. Bowling Green: Popular Press, 1981.

"The Broad Regions of a Writer's Life." *Chicago Sun-Times* (August 12, 1979).

"The Left-Handedness of Modern Literature." *Twentieth-Century Literature* 23, no. 4 (December 1977).

"Invisible Men and Women: The Disappearance of Character in Science Fiction." *Science-Fiction Studies* 4, no. 1 (March 1977). In Ryszard Handke et al., *Spor o SF.* Poznan, Poland: Wydawnictwo Poznanskie, 1989 (Polish translation).

"Marxism and the Writing of Fiction." *Minnesota Review,* new series, no. 5 (Fall 1975).

"Pynchon's Paranoid History." *Twentieth-Century Literature* 21, no. 2 (May 1975).

"An Interview with Stanley Elkin." *Contemporary Literature* 16, no. 2 (Spring 1975).

"Towards a Social Theory of Literature." *Telos* 18 (Winter 1973–74).

SOUND RECORDINGS

Reading. *Live from Prairie Lights*. WSUI-FM, Iowa City, Iowa, March 6, 1998.

Interviewed by Bob Willard. *Profiles*. WFIU-FM, Bloomington, Indiana, December 20, 1998.

Interviewed by Michael Silverblatt with Robert Michael Pyle. *Bookworm*. KCRW-Public Radio, Los Angeles, California, April 17, 1996.

Interviewed by Bill Dudley. Florida Public Radio, Seaside, Florida, May 6, 1995.

Reading. University of Arizona, Tucson, Arizona, April 3, 1995 (Orion Society).

"Conversations." Interviewed by Susan McKinnis. KUAC-FM, Fairbanks, Alaska, March 17, 1994.

Interview. Wisconsin Public Radio, Madison, Wisconsin, September 14, 1993.

"Down to Earth." Interview. WFPL-FM, Louisville, Kentucky, April 11, 1993.

Interviewed by Margaret Joseph. WFIU-FM, Bloomington, Indiana, December 15, 1985.

Interview. *Profiles*. WFIU-FM, Bloomington, Indiana, October 6, 1983.

VIDEO RECORDINGS

Reading and interview. Lannan Foundation, Los Angeles, California, May 20, 1997.

Interviewed by Roy Harvey. *Chicago Books*. Public Access Station, Chicago, Illinois, February 26, 1996.

Interview. *Studio 6.* WTIU (Public Broadcasting System affiliate), Bloomington, Indiana, June 17, 1993.

Interview. *Studio 6.* WTIU (Public Broadcasting System affiliate), Bloomington, Indiana, January 9, 1992.

Reading. Prairie Lights Bookstore. Iowa Public Television, Iowa City, Iowa, October 5, 1990.

ANTHOLOGY APPEARANCES

"Beauty." *The Best American Essays 1999,* edited by Edward Hoagland and Robert Atwan. Boston: Houghton Mifflin, 1999.

"Buckeye." *Literature and the Environment: A Reader on Nature and Culture,* edited by Lorraine Anderson, Scott Slovic, and John P. O'Grady. New York: Addison Wesley Longman, 1999.

"Cloud Crossing" and "The Singular First Person." *The Fourth Genre: Contemporary Writers of/on Creative Nonfiction.* New York: Allyn and Bacon, 1998.

"Digging Limestone." *The Riverside Reader,* edited by Joseph Trimmer and Maxine Hairston. 6th ed. Boston: Houghton Mifflin, 1998.

"The Inheritance of Tools." *The Prentice-Hall Reader,* edited by George Miller. 5th ed. New York: Simon & Schuster, 1998.

"The Men We Carry in Our Minds." *Bedford Guide for College Writers,* edited by X. J. Kennedy et al. 5th ed. Boston: Bedford Books, 1998.

"Silence." *Falling Toward Grace: Images of Religion and Culture from the Heartland,* edited by J. Kent

Calder and Susan Neville. Bloomington: Indiana
University Press, 1998.

"To Eva, on Your Marriage." *Fathering Daughters:
Reflections by Men,* edited by DeWitt Henry and
James Alan McPherson. Boston: Beacon, 1998.

"Buckeye." *American Nature Writing 1997,* edited by
John A. Murray. San Francisco: Sierra Club Books,
1997.

"Doing Time in the Thirteenth Chair." *Affinities:
Readings in Common,* edited by Wendolyn Tetlow
and Martin Gloege. New York: Simon & Schuster,
1997.

"Earth's Body." *Transitions: Lives in America,* edited
by Irina Raicu and Greg Grewel. New York: West
Publishing, 1997.

"The Inheritance of Tools." *The Norton Book of
Personal Essays,* edited by Joseph Epstein. New
York: Norton, 1997.

"Looking at Women." *Reading and Writing from
Literature,* edited by John Schweibert. Boston:
Houghton Mifflin, 1997.

"The Men We Carry in Our Minds." *Critical Issues
in Contemporary Cultures,* edited by Eleanor
McKenna. New York: Allyn and Bacon, 1997.

"A Perfect Place." *Family: A Twenty-Fifth Anniversary
Collection of Essays about the Family from Notre
Dame Magazine,* edited by Kerry Temple. Notre
Dame: University of Notre Dame Press, 1997.

"The Web of Life." *The Bedford Reader,* edited by X. J.
Kennedy et al. 6th ed. Boston: Bedford Books,
1997.

"Amos and James." *Communion: Contemporary*

Writers Reveal the Bible in Their Lives, edited by
David Rosenberg. New York: Anchor, 1996.

"Buckeye." *The Sacred Place: Witnessing the Holy in the
Physical World,* edited by W. Scott Olsen and Scott
Cairns. Salt Lake City: University of Utah Press,
1996.

"The Common Life." *Rooted in the Land: Essays on
Community and Place,* edited by William Vitek and
Wes Jackson. New Haven: Yale University Press,
1996.

"Death Games." *Changing the Bully Who Rules the
World,* edited by Carol Bly. Minneapolis:
Milkweed Editions, 1996.

"The Men We Carry in Our Minds." *A Community of
Readers,* edited by Roberta Alexander and Jan
Lombardi. New York: Harper Collins, 1996.

"The Men We Carry in Our Minds." *Experiencing
America: Identity, Power and Change,* edited by
Virginia J. Cyrus. New York: Mayfield, 1996.

"Mountain Music." *The Place Within: Portraits of the
American Landscape by Twenty Contemporary
Writers,* edited by Jodi Daynard. New York:
Norton, 1996.

"Reasons of the Body." *In a Dark Wood,* edited by
Steven Harvey. Athens: University of Georgia
Press, 1996.

"Speaking a Word for Nature." *The Ecocriticism
Reader,* edited by Cheryll Glotfelty and Harold
Fromm. Athens: University of Georgia Press,
1996.

"Wayland." *Encounters: Readings and the World,*
edited by Pat Hoy II and Robert DiYanni. New
York: McGraw Hill, 1996.

"Digging Limestone." *The Riverside Reader,* edited by Joseph Trimmer and Maxine C. Hairston. 5th ed. Boston: Houghton Mifflin, 1995.

"Doing Time in the Thirteenth Chair." *The Contemporary Essay,* edited by Donald Hall. 3rd ed. Boston: Bedford/St. Martin's, 1995.

"Ground Notes." *Magazine Feature Writing,* edited by Rick Wilber. New York: St. Martin's, 1995.

"Looking at Women" and "Under the Influence." *The Norton Reader,* edited by Linda H. Peterson et al. 9th ed. New York: Norton, 1995.

"The Men We Carry in Our Minds." *The Little, Brown Reader,* edited by Sylvan Barnet and Marcia Stubbs. 7th ed. New York: Little, Brown, 1995.

"Fathers, Sons, Sports." *Horizons,* edited by Ken Roy. Toronto: Harcourt Brace Canada, 1994.

"The Inheritance of Tools." *The Best American Essays for College Students,* edited by Robert Atwan. Boston: Houghton Mifflin, 1994.

"The Inheritance of Tools." *Writing with a Purpose,* edited by Joseph Trimmer. Boston: Houghton Mifflin, 1994.

"The Men We Carry in Our Minds." *Common Ground,* edited by Laurie G. Kirszner and Stephen R. Mandell. New York: St Martin's, 1994.

"The Men We Carry in Our Minds." *The Writer's Presence,* edited by Donald McQuade and Robert Atwan. Boston: Bedford/St. Martin's, 1994.

"Settling Down." *A Forest of Voices,* edited by Lex Runcimen and Chris Anderson. New York: Mayfield, 1994.

"Under the Influence." *The Art of the Personal Essay,* edited by Phillip Lopate. New York: Anchor, 1994.

"Under the Influence." *Cartographies: Contemporary American Essays*, edited by Diana Young. Boston: Bedford/St. Martin's, 1994.

"Voyageurs." *The Nature of Nature*, edited by William H. Shore. New York: Harcourt Brace, 1994.

"The Inheritance of Tools" and "The Men We Carry in Our Minds." *Inquiries*, edited by Lynn Z. Bloom and Edward M. White. New York: Simon & Schuster, 1993.

"The Inheritance of Tools." *Windows*, edited by Rackham and Bertagnolli. New York: Harper Collins, 1993.

"Lady Chatterley's Loving and the Annihilation Impulse." *Twentieth-Century Literary Criticism*, edited by Laurie DiMauro. Detroit: Gale Research, 1993.

"The Men We Carry in Our Minds." *The Bedford Guide for College Writers*, edited by X. J. Kennedy et al. 3rd ed. Boston: St. Martin's, 1993.

"The Men We Carry in Our Minds." *The Essay, Old and New*, edited by P. J. Corbett and Sheryl L. Finkle. New York: Blair Press, 1993.

"The Men We Carry in Our Minds." *The Little, Brown Reader*, edited by Sylvan Barnet and Marcia Stubbs. 6th ed. New York: Little, Brown, 1993.

"Reasons of the Body." *The Dolphin Reader*, edited by Douglas Hunt. 3rd ed. Boston: Houghton Mifflin, 1993.

"The Singular First Person," "Cloud Crossing," and "Listening to Owls." *Being in the World: An Environmental Reader for Writers*, edited by Scott H. Slovic and Terrell F. Dixon. New York: Macmillan, 1993.

"Under the Influence." *Turning Toward Home: Reflections on the Family from Harper's Magazine.* New York: Franklin Square/Harper's, 1993.

"Wayland." *The Best American Essays 1993,* edited by Joseph Epstein. New York: Ticknor & Fields, 1993.

"The Inheritance of Tools." *The Prentice-Hall Reader,* edited by George Miller. 3rd ed. New York: Simon & Schuster, 1992.

"Looking at Women" and "The Singular First Person." *The Norton Reader,* edited by Arthur M. Eastman et al. 8th ed. New York: Norton, 1992.

"The Men We Carry in Our Minds." *The Blair Reader,* edited by Lauri G. Kirszner and Stephen R. Mandell. New York: Simon & Schuster, 1992.

"The Men We Carry in Our Minds." *The Borzoi College Reader,* edited by Charles Muscatine and Marlene Griffith. 7th ed. New York: McGraw Hill, 1992.

"The Philosophical Cobbler." *Flash Fiction: Seventy-Two Very Short Stories,* edited by James Thomas et al. New York: Norton, 1992.

"Tokens of Mystery." *Finding Home,* edited by Peter Sauer. Boston: Beacon, 1992.

"Doing Time in the Thirteenth Chair." *The Art of the Essay,* edited by Lydia Fakundiny. Boston: Houghton Mifflin, 1991.

"The Force of Moving Water." *Always a River: The Ohio River and the American Experience,* edited by Robert L. Reid. Bloomington: Indiana University Press, 1991.

"The Inheritance of Tools." *The Harper and Row Reader,* edited by Wayne Booth and Marshall Gregory. 3rd ed. New York: Harper and Row, 1991.

"The Men We Carry in Our Minds." *The Winchester Reader,* edited by Donald McQuade. Boston: Bedford, 1991.

"Speaking a Word for Nature." *Writers and Their Craft,* edited by Nicholas Delbanco and Laurence Goldstein. Detroit: Wayne State University Press, 1991.

"Under the Influence" and "The Inheritance of Tools." *The Essay Connection: Readings for Writers,* edited by Lynn Z. Bloom. 3rd ed. Lexington, Mass.: D. C. Heath, 1991.

"Digging Limestone" and "The Inheritance of Tools." *The Riverside Reader,* edited by Joseph F. Trimmer. 3rd ed. Boston: Houghton Mifflin, 1990.

"The Inheritance of Tools." *The New Harvest Reader,* edited by William Heffernan et al. New York: Harcourt Brace Jovanovich, 1990.

"The First Journey of Jason Moss." *New Territory,* edited by Michael Wilkerson and Deborah Galyan. Bloomington: Indiana University Press, 1990.

"Living Souls." *Openings: Original Essays by Contemporary Soviet and American Writers,* edited by Robert Atwan and Valeri Vinokurov. Seattle: University of Washington, 1990.

"The Operation." *Vital Lines: Contemporary Fiction about Medicine,* edited by Jon Mukand. New York: St. Martin's, 1990.

"At Play in the Paradise of Bombs." *The Dolphin Reader,* edited by Douglas Hunt. 2nd ed. Boston: Houghton Mifflin, 1989.

"Death Games." *Our Times,* edited by Robert Atwan. Boston: Bedford, 1989.

"Doing Time in the Thirteenth Chair." *The*

Contemporary Essay, edited by Donald Hall.
2nd ed. New York: St. Martin's, 1989.

"The Inheritance of Tools." *The Prentice-Hall Reader,*
edited by George Miller. 2nd ed. New York: Simon
& Schuster, 1989.

"Landscape and Imagination." *Where We Live,* edited
by David Hoppe. Bloomington: Indiana University
Press, 1989.

"The Singular First Person." *Essays on the Essay,* edited
by Alexander J. Butrym. Athens: University of
Georgia Press, 1989.

"Speaking a Word for Nature." *Contemporary
American Fiction,* edited by Nicholas Delbanco
and Lawrence Goldstein. Detroit: Wayne State
University Press, 1989.

"Listening to Owls." *The Norton Reader,* edited by
Arthur M. Eastman et al. 7th ed. New York:
Norton, 1988.

"Nature versus Society in *The Rainbow.*" *Modern
Critical Interpretations: "The Rainbow,"* edited by
Harold Bloom. New Haven: Chelsea House, 1988.

"The Inheritance of Tools." *The Best American Essays
1987,* edited by Gay Talese and Robert Atwan.
New York: Ticknor & Fields, 1987.

"America Is One Long Bloody Fight." *Georgia Review:
Fortieth Anniversary Fiction Retrospective* 40, no. 1
(Spring 1986).

"The Anatomy Lesson." *One Hundred Great Fantasy
Short Stories,* edited by Isaac Asimov. Garden City,
N.Y.: Doubleday, 1984.

"The Cold," "Healing Waters," "The Wandering of
Lake Erie," "Hermit," "Bones," "The Indians Win
Another One," and "Frostbite on the Soul." *Ohio*

Review: Ten Year Retrospective, no. 30 (Summer 1983).

"The Anatomy Lesson." *Aliens and Outworlders,* edited by Shawna McCarthy. New York: Dial Press, 1983.

INTERVIEWS

Lee, Jeff. "Honoring the Given World: An Interview with Scott Russell Sanders." *Stone Crop* (Summer 1997).

Perry, Carolyn, and Wayne Zade. "Something Durable and Whole: An Interview with Scott Russell Sanders." *Kenyon Review* (Fall 1999).

Root, Robert L. "An Interview with Scott Russell Sanders." *Fourth Genre* 1, no. 1 (Spring 1999).

Zirker, Joan McTigue, "A Meeting of Midwestern Minds." Joint interview with Frank Popoff. *College* (Spring 1996).

BIOGRAPHICAL/CRITICAL STUDIES AND BOOK REVIEWS

Babener, Liana. Review of *Writing from the Center. Choice* (February 1996).

Broderick, Kathryn. Review of *Warm as Wool. Booklist* (November 15, 1992).

Burghard, Sharon Laws. "When Poetic Becomes Rhetoric: Mythic Re-vision as Feminist Rhetorical Tool." *A Ribbon at a Time: A Collection of Personal Essays.* D. A. dissertation, Idaho State University, 1994.

Burns, Mary M. Review of *Aurora Means Dawn. Horn Book Magazine* (September/October 1989).

Calderazzo, John. "How to Write the Personal Essay." *Writer's Digest* (May 1995).

Campbell, Patty. Review of *Staying Put. Wilson Library Bulletin* (September 1993).

Caywood, Carolyn. Review of *The Engineer of Beasts. Journal of Reading* (December 1989).

Curtis, Christopher Paul. Review of *A Place Called Freedom. New York Times Book Review* (June 22, 1997).

Eastburn, Kathryn. "Putting Down Roots." Review of *Writing from the Center. Colorado Springs Independent* 4, no. 50 (1996).

Fakih, Kimberly Olson, and Diane Roback. Review of *Aurora Means Dawn. Publishers Weekly* (June 30, 1989).

———. Review of *The Engineer of Beasts. Publishers Weekly* (October 14, 1988).

Farmer, Lesley S. J. Review of *The Engineer of Beasts. Wilson Library Bulletin* (September 1989).

Gilbert, Richard. "Scott Russell Sanders: A Sense of Place." *Bloomington Herald-Times* (January 12, 1986).

Gundy, Jeff. Review of *Staying Put. Georgia Review* (Summer 1994).

Hanson, Susan. Review of *Staying Put. San Marcos (Texas) Daily Record* (May 23, 1993).

———. Review of *Writing from the Center. San Marcos (Texas) Daily Record* (February 4, 1996).

Heilker, Paul. *Rehabilitating the Essay: An Alternative Form for Composition Instruction.* Ph.D. dissertation, Texas Christian University, 1992.

Hoppe, David. "Down to Earth in the Midwest: Scott

Russell Sanders and *Writing from the Center.*" *Traces* (Spring 1996).

Kaufman, James. "Essayist: 'We Already Dwell in the Place Worth Seeking.'" *Des Moines Register* (January 28, 1996).

Laughner, Nissa. "Balancing: A Profile of Scott Russell Sanders." *Hiram College* (Winter 1997).

Lichtenberg, Carol J. Review of *The Paradise of Bombs. Library Journal* (April 1, 1987).

Lueders, Edward. Review of *Secrets of the Universe. Southern Review* (Spring 1992).

Markus, Tim. Review of *Staying Put. Library Journal* (May 15, 1993).

Melton, Emily. Review of *Here Comes the Mystery Man. Booklist* (November 15, 1993).

Nash, Susan Smith. Review of *Secrets of the Universe. Georgia Review* (Winter 1992).

Nelson, Ronald J. "The Nature Writing of Scott Russell Sanders." *Professional Communication Society Newsletter* 41, no. 1 (January/February 1997).

Neville, Susan. "On Wildness and Domesticity." *Arts Indiana* (October 1993).

Nichols, William. "Environmentalism and the Legitimacy of Hope." Review of *Writing from the Center. Kenyon Review* (Summer/Fall 1996).

———. "Scott Russell Sanders." *American Nature Writers*. Vol. 2. Edited by John Elder. New York: Scribner's, 1996.

Nicolini, Mary B. "Scott Russell Sanders: Wrestling with the Fine Line." *Arts Indiana* (December 1987).

Parrinder, Patrick. "Swan-Songs: The Novels of Scott

R. Sanders." *Poetry Nation Review* 14, no. 3 (December 1987).

Poyser, Jim. "Living Inside Scott Russell Sanders' Life." *Bloomington Voice* 4, no. 18 (April 26–May 3, 1995).

———. "Stealing Time from Writer Scott Russell Sanders: All Booked Up." *Arts Indiana* 17, no. 7 (October 1995).

Randall, Lynn. Review of *Secrets of the Universe. Publishers Weekly* (October 4, 1991).

Review of *Here Comes the Mystery Man. Publishers Weekly* (July 26, 1993).

Review of *Hunting for Hope. Booklist* (September 1, 1998).

Review of *Hunting for Hope. Publishers Weekly* (August 10, 1998).

Review of *Hunting for Hope. Values and Visions Reviews Service* (September 10, 1998).

Review of *A Place Called Freedom. Publishers Weekly* (May 19, 1997).

Review of *Staying Put. Publishers Weekly* (April 26, 1993).

Review of *Writing from the Center. Christian Science Monitor* (October 26, 1995).

Review of *Writing from the Center. Los Angeles Times Book Review* (October 29, 1995).

Review of *Writing from the Center. Publishers Weekly* (August 21, 1995).

Review of *Writing from the Center. School Library Journal* (February 1996).

Rueter, Thad. "Leader by Trade, Writer by Heart." *LUX* (February 9, 1996).

Ryden, Kent C. *Mapping the Invisible Landscape:*

Folklore, Writing, and the Sense of Place. Iowa City: University of Iowa Press, 1993.

Scholfield, Randy Todd. *Finding Native Ground: Essays on American Nature Writing.* Ph.D. dissertation, University of Kansas, 1996.

Shires, Nancy. Review of *Writing from the Center. Library Journal* (September 1, 1995).

Taylor, Robert. "For Sanders, Hope Springs from Reason." Review of *Hunting for Hope. Boston Globe* (October 6, 1998).

Trimnel, Angus. Review of *Staying Put. Booklist* (June 1, 1993).

Vasilakis, Nancy. Review of *The Engineer of Beasts. Horn Book Magazine* (September/October 1988).

Walzer, Kevin. "Staying Put: The Invisible Landscape of Scott Russell Sanders's Nonfiction." *Journal of Kentucky Studies* (1994).

Weisman, Kay. Review of *A Place Called Freedom. Booklist* (June 1, 1997).

———. Review of *The Floating House. Booklist* (June 1, 1995).

Wheeler, David L. "A Quarrel with His Son Prompts a Writer to Meditate on Hope." Review of *Hunting for Hope. Chronicle of Higher Education* (October 2, 1998).

Wilson, Steve. "Cult of the Individual Weakens Sense of Community." *Arizona Republic* (September 15, 1996).

Zender, Anne. "Telling the Stories of Ordinary Life." *Indiana Alumni* (January/February 1993).

ACKNOWLEDGMENTS FOR
"THE COUNTRY OF LANGUAGE"

by Scott Russell Sanders

As I say briefly in the dedication to this volume, I am grateful to all my teachers, living and dead, in school and out, those I've met in the flesh and those I've met only through books. The earliest of these teachers were my father and mother, Greeley Ray Sanders and Eva Mary Solomon Sanders; and then my sister, Sandra, and my brother, Glenn; and then the underpaid but dedicated teachers at Charlestown Elementary and Southeast High School in Portage County, Ohio, above all Eugene Fahnert and Fay Givens. From my professors at Brown University I am especially indebted to George Morgan, Edward Ahearn, Wendell Dietrich, and Mark Spilka. From those at Cambridge University, I recall with greatest affection T. R. Henn and Raymond Williams. From my many inspiring colleagues at Indiana University, let me mention Donald Gray, who is an exemplary man.

Any good teaching—how to read and write, how to play a banjo, how to bake bread—is a passing on of gifts. I have received gifts from more people than I could possibly name. I bless them all.

WORKS CITED

p. 91   Scott Russell Sanders, *Writing from the Center* (Bloomington: Indiana University Press, 1995), 69–70.

p. 92   Scott Russell Sanders, *The Paradise of Bombs* (Athens: University of Georgia Press, 1987), xiii.

p. 93   Scott Russell Sanders, *The Paradise of Bombs,* xiv.

p. 94   Jeff Lee, "Honoring the Given World: An Interview with Scott Russell Sanders," *Stone Crop: A Natural History Book Catalog* (Summer 1997): 29.

p. 94   Scott Russell Sanders, *Secrets of the Universe: Scenes from the Journey Home* (Boston: Beacon, 1991), 226–27.

p. 95   Henry David Thoreau, *Walden* (1854; reprint, Princeton: Princeton University Press, 1971), 3.

p. 95   Scott Russell Sanders, *The Paradise of Bombs,* xv.

p. 96   Scott Russell Sanders, *Secrets of the Universe,* 191.

p. 96   Scott Russell Sanders, "From Anonymous, Evasive Prose to Writing with Passion," *Chronicle of Higher Education* (October 10, 1997): B4.

p. 97   Scott Russell Sanders, "From Anonymous, Evasive Prose to Writing with Passion," B5.

p. 97   Scott Russell Sanders, "From Anonymous, Evasive Prose to Writing with Passion," B5.

pp. 97–98   Scott Russell Sanders, Alison Hawthorne Deming, and Richard Nelson, letter to *Orion* readers, *Orion* (Autumn 1995): 5.

pp. 99–100 Scott Russell Sanders, *Staying Put: Making a Home in a Restless World* (Boston: Beacon, 1993), 12.

p. 100   Scott Russell Sanders, *Writing from the Center,* 173.

pp. 103–4 Scott Russell Sanders, *Terrarium* (1985; reprint, Bloomington: Indiana University Press, 1995), 278.

p. 104   Scott Russell Sanders, *Secrets of the Universe,* 190.

p. 104   Scott Russell Sanders, *Writing from the Center,* 13.

pp. 104–5 Scott Russell Sanders, *Staying Put,* 149.

p. 105   Scott Russell Sanders, *Staying Put,* 169.

p. 105   Scott Russell Sanders, *Hunting for Hope: A Father's Journeys* (Boston: Beacon, 1998), 9.

p. 106   Scott Russell Sanders, *Hunting for Hope,* 188.

SCOTT SLOVIC, founding president of the Association for the Study of Literature and Environment (ASLE), currently serves as editor of the journal *ISLE: Interdisciplinary Studies in Literature and Environment.* He is the author of *Seeking Awareness in American Nature Writing: Henry Thoreau, Annie Dillard, Edward Abbey, Wendell Berry, Barry Lopez* (University of Utah Press, 1992); his coedited books include *Being in the World: An Environmental Reader for Writers* (Macmillan, 1993), *Reading the Earth: New Directions in the Study of Literature and the Environment* (University of Idaho Press, 1998), and *Literature and the Environment: A Reader on Nature and Culture* (Addison Wesley Longman, 1999). Currently he is an associate professor of English and the director of the Center for Environmental Arts and Humanities at the University of Nevada, Reno.

Brown Dog of the Yaak:
Essays on Art and Activism
Rick Bass

Boundary Waters:
The Grace of the Wild
Paul Gruchow

Grass Roots:
The Universe of Home
Paul Gruchow

The Necessity of Empty Places
Paul Gruchow

A Sense of the Morning:
Field Notes of a Born Observer
David Brendan Hopes

Taking Care:
Thoughts on Storytelling and Belief
William Kittredge

Ecology of a Cracker Childhood
Janisse Ray

The Dream of the Marsh Wren:
Writing As Reciprocal Creation
Pattiann Rogers

The Book of the Tongass
Edited by Carolyn Servid and Donald Snow

Homestead
Annick Smith

Testimony:
Writers of the West Speak On Behalf of Utah Wilderness
Compiled by Stephen Trimble
and Terry Tempest Williams

OTHER BOOKS OF INTEREST TO
THE WORLD AS HOME READER:

Essays

The Heart Can Be Filled Anywhere on Earth:
Minneota, Minnesota
Bill Holm

Shedding Life:
Disease, Politics, and Other Human Conditions
Miroslav Holub

Children's Novels

No Place
Kay Haugaard

The Monkey Thief
Aileen Kilgore Henderson

Treasure of Panther Peak
Aileen Kilgore Henderson

The Dog with Golden Eyes
Frances Wilbur

Anthologies

Sacred Ground:
Writings about Home
Edited by Barbara Bonner

Verse and Universe:
Poems about Science and Mathematics
Edited by Kurt Brown

Poetry

Boxelder Bug Variations
Bill Holm

Butterfly Effect
Harry Humes

Eating Bread and Honey
Pattiann Rogers

Firekeeper:
New and Selected Poems
Pattiann Rogers

THE WORLD AS HOME, the nonfiction publishing program of Milkweed Editions, is dedicated to exploring our relationship to the natural world. Not espousing any particular environmentalist or political agenda, these books are a forum for distinctive literary writing that not only alerts the reader to vital issues but offers personal testimonies to living harmoniously with other species in urban, rural, and wilderness communities.

MILKWEED EDITIONS publishes with the intention of making a humane impact on society, in the belief that literature is a transformative art uniquely able to convey the essential experiences of the human heart and spirit. To that end, Milkweed publishes distinctive voices of literary merit in handsomely designed, visually dynamic books, exploring the ethical, cultural, and esthetic issues that free societies need continually to address. Milkweed Editions is a not-for-profit press.

Typeset in Stone Serif
by Stanton Publication Services, Inc.
Printed on acid-free, recycled
55# Frasier Miami Book Natural paper
by Friesen Corporation